The Unconscious Christian

James A. Hall, M.D.

The Unconscious Christian

IMAGES OF GOD IN DREAMS

edited by
Daniel J. Meckel

Paulist Press
New York ◇ Mahwah

Library of Congress Cataloging-in-Publication Data

Hall, James A. (James Albert), 1934–
   The unconscious Christian: images of God in dreams/by James A.
Hall; edited by Daniel J. Meckel.
      p. cm.—(Jung and spirituality)
   Includes bibliographical references.
   ISBN 0-8091-3353-9
   1. Image of God. 2. Dreams—Religious aspects—Christianity.
3. Christianity—Psychology. 4. Psychoanalysis and religion.
I. Meckel, Daniel J. II. Title. III. Series.
BT102.H33   1992
248.2'01'9—dc20   92-26395
                                                 CIP

Published by Paulist Press
997 Macarthur Blvd.
Mahwah, N.J. 07430

Contents

SERIES FOREWORD

The *Jung and Spirituality* series provides a forum for the critical interaction between Jungian psychology and living spiritual traditions. The series serves two important goals.

The first goal is: *To enhance a creative exploration of the contributions and criticisms which Jung's psychology can offer to religion.* Jungian thought has far-reaching implications for the understanding and practice of spirituality. Interest in these implications continues to expand in both Christian and non-Christian religious communities. People are increasingly aware of the depth and insight which a Jungian perspective adds to the human experiences of the sacred. And yet, the use of Jungian psychoanalysis clearly does not eliminate the need for careful philosophical, theological and ethical reflection or for maintaining one's centeredness in a spiritual tradition.

The second goal is: *To bring the creative insights and critical tools of religious studies and practice to bear on Jungian thought.* Many volumes in the Jung and Spirituality series work to define the borders of the Jungian and spiritual traditions, to bring the spiritual dimensions of Jung's work into relief, and to deepen those dimensions. We believe that an important outcome of the Jung-Spirituality dialogue is greater cooperation of psychology and spirituality. Such cooperation will move us ahead in the formation of a post-modern spirituality, equal to the challenges of the twenty-first century.

Robert L. Moore
Series Editor

Daniel J. Meckel
Managing Editor

DEDICATION

To the Memory of Albert Outler,
a wise man and a friend.

ACKNOWLEDGMENTS

The editor and publisher have made every effort to determine and credit the holders of copyright of the materials reproduced in this book. Any errors or omissions may be rectified in future volumes. The editor and publisher wish to thank the following for permission to reproduce the following materials: Clyde E. Keeler for permission to reproduce the sketch of Achusimmutupalit shown on page 63 of Clyde E. Keeler's *Cuña Indian Art* published by Exposition Press, New York, copyright (c) C.E. Keeler, 1969. Museo Archeologico Nazionale, Napoli, Italy, for permission to use a photograph of the statue of Ephesian Artemis, made of alabaster, gilt and bronze, dating from the time of Hadrian. Monumenti Musei E. Gallerie Pontificie, Vatican City, Italy, for permission to reproduce "Aklamenes sculpture of Aesculapius." National-galerie, Berlin, Germany, for permission to use the painting by Peter Cornelius entitled *Joseph Interprets Pharaoh's Dreams*, dated to the period 1815–1817. Ministry of Culture, Antiquities Organization, Egyptian Museum, Cairo, Egypt, for permission to reproduce a photograph of the goddess Taweret. The British Library, London, England, for permission to reproduce the following: a detail of St. Swithin's Psalter, fol. 9r., "The Tree of Jesse," used on the cover of this book, and a photograph of the scroll entitled "Anubis and the Weighing of the Heart," from the Papyrus of Hunifer (Egyptian, circa 1310) (papyrus no. 9901, scene 125d). Bibliotheque de l'Arsenal, Paris, France, for permission to reproduce a photograph of the illustration of an alchemical vessel sealed with a small sphere and containing at the bottom a pelican piercing its breast with its beak, from the manuscript *De Summa et universalis medicinae sapientiae*, fol. 39, fig. 37. Bibliotheque Nationale, Paris, France, for permission to reproduce the photograph of "Uroborus," from *Livre Sur L'Art De Faire De L'Or* and also for permission to reproduce the photograph, "Crucifie," from *Christ Crucifie* (Latin 2246). The Asian Art Museum of San Francisco, The Avery Brundage Collection, San Francisco, California, for permission to reproduce a photograph B65 S5, Maya's Dream. Sigmund Freud Copyrights, by permission of A. W. Freud, et al. for permission to use photograph No. 1506. *Paulist Press acknowledges use of materials from the following institutions:* Government Central Museum, Albert Hall, Ramniwas Gardens, Jaipur, India, for use of a photograph of the sandstone relief of Ardhanarisvara: The Lord Whose Half Is Woman, dating from the ninth century, originally located in a Shaivite temple. Sarnath Museum, Varanasi, India, for the reproduction of a picture of the high-relief sculpture, in buff Chunar sandstone, of the first preaching of the Buddha (ca. 475 A.D.). Musée d'Unterlinden, Colmar, France, for the reproduction of a photograph of "The Crucifixion," a detail from the Isenheim Altarpiece by Mathias Grunewald. Municipal Museum, Guan Di Miao Temple, Henan Province, People's Republic of China, for the reproduction of a photograph of the Vairocana Buddha (of the longmen caves). National Gallery, Trafalgar Square, London, England, for the reproduction of a photograph of "The Virgin and Child before a Firescreen," attributed to Robert Campin. Museo Nacional del Prado, Madrid, Spain, for the reproduction of a photograph of the painting "The River Styx," signed by Joachim Patinir. Musée Granet, Bouches-du-Rhone, France, for the reproduction of a painting by Ingres entitled "Jupiter and Thetis," painted in 1811.

Editor's Foreword

When Dr. James Hall proposed to write a book on divine images in dreams for the *Jung and Spirituality* series, we were understandably delighted. An outstanding authority on the Jungian interpretation of dreams, his works have provided countless persons with entry and passage through this fascinating realm. In our early conversations about this volume, Hall proposed to base his work, *The Unconscious Christian*, on Jung's assumption that anyone raised in the western world, whether or not they profess to be religious, is inevitably and unconsciously shaped by western religions. Religious and moral concerns that run deep in the flow of modern culture may be repressed but not banished from the psyche. They will inevitably make their appearance, Hall argues, and exert their influence through the symbolism of fantasy and dreams. In addition, those who do carry a conscious religious identity will discover in their dreams, if they look closely, religious images and meanings which hearken far beyond the borders of their own conscious traditions.

Professor Robert Moore and I wholeheartedly approved James Hall's proposed volume, which draws from his years of clinical experience and reflection upon the significance of religious images in dreams. Hall's discussions in this volume expand upon some of his previous articles. They include: "Religious Images in Dreams" (1979); "Psychiatry and Religion: a Review and a Projection of Future Needs" (1981); "Jungian

1

Theory in Religious Counseling" (1980); and "The Work of J.B. Rhine: Implications for Religion" (1981). The question of a natural religious function in the psyche (treated in the appendix) was discussed in London in 1987 in a presentation by Dr. Hall to Gerhard Adler's training group.

Regrettably, in the early phases of preparation, Dr. Hall became seriously ill and was not able to complete the work himself. In consultation with him, I have edited and shaped the material into its present form, and included several photographs and figures. These, I hope, will enhance and clarify Hall's descriptions as he guides the reader through the basic elements of Jungian dream interpretation, and examines a panoply of divine figures encountered in his patients' and his own dreams.

I would personally like to thank Robert Moore (General Editor of the series) for his much needed advice and support during the editing of this book. Special thanks go out to the *Jung Institute of San Francisco* and especially to Michael Flanagin, Curator of the *Archive for Research in Archetypal Symbolism* in San Francisco. Michael's highly informed and friendly assistance has been essential to the "creative imaging" of this volume. I am also grateful to Laura Praglin, whose editorial expertise has been indispensable.

Above all, I would like to offer my respect and thanks to Dr. James A. Hall for his continuing work on dream interpretation. I hope that the present volume will bring his creative efforts before an even larger audience.

Daniel J. Meckel
Managing Editor,
Jung and Spirituality Series

Preface

For a number of years I served as a clinical consultant to the internship program of Perkins School of Theology, Southern Methodist University, in Dallas. In that capacity I met several times a month with six to eight pastoral interns in a "growth group" format, very much like abbreviated group psychotherapy. I met on a less frequent basis with the pastors to whose churches the interns were assigned. These pastors served as supervisors of the interns' work, and their approval was necessary for an intern to pass the internship program. The year of internship was required for the ordination into the Methodist Church in this conference, and also for ordination of many students of other denominations who attended Perkins.

At the end of each semester, I met with each intern, the committee of six to eight members of the church the intern served, the supervising pastor of the intern, and a representative of the Perkins faculty who was the field instructor responsible for overseeing the "field unit" that included all the interns in my care, as well as those of one or two other consultants. A satisfactory semester evaluation served as a major part of the overall evaluation of the intern's completed work.

My motivation for participation in this program was partially religious. I had grown up in the Methodist Church and for one year in high school was president of the Methodist Youth Fellowship in the Texas conference. Although no longer affiliated with a particular congregation, I still felt a sense of loyalty to the Methodist tradition and concern for its ongoing development.

I had also greatly benefited from the friendship and conversation of the late Albert Outler, a renowned Methodist theologian who, with myself, Harville Hendrix and James Gwaltney (both then on the Perkins faculty) had been a founder of the Isthmus Institute, a Dallas organization that sponsors yearly dialogues on the convergence of science and religion. My other motive for participating for many years in the internship program was the example of my close colleague and friend, Gladys Guy Brown, co-therapist with me in group psychotherapy for over twenty years. Dr. Brown had devoted a great deal of time to the Perkins intern program. I had hoped to understand, from first-hand observation, how the religious impulse in ministers in training worked itself out in the persons I would observe. And, of course, I hoped to contribute in some way to the improvement of the program.

The dedication, humility, and true religious calling of the interns whom I saw during these years impressed me. In the growth groups, I was amazed time and again at the virtual leaps that some interns made in their own psychological growth and health. In some cases this seemed to me the result of a religious conversion experience, a deep emotional revaluing, and an increased sense of humility. The interns who experienced this usually believed that they had felt intuitively the presence of a divine reality greater than the ego-personality. This type of experience seemed to produce a lasting change in the personality of the intern.

There were also some disappointments and, in some cases, a severe psychological problem could be identified. Unfortunately, the amount of time allotted for the groups and the fact that they were composed of fellow students who were often friends, was not conducive to uncovering and working-through any deep psychological problems.

In one instance, the intern, with the apparent collusion of a supervising pastor, refused to face the psychopathology that the growth group experience had revealed in him. When I arrived at the church for the semester evaluation of this intern with his committee, the field instructor and I were surprised to find a table decorated for a party celebration, complete with cake and punch. It proved impossible in that atmosphere to deal effectively with the quite serious psychopathology of the intern, which surfaced only after several years into his ministry.

After several years of work with the Perkins program, another incident occurred which I sometimes refer to as a "horror story." It revealed the current sad state of affairs in understanding and using dreams containing potential religious meanings. An intern was having difficulty speaking up to his supervising pastor, a religious fundamentalist, about certain personality difficulties he felt had come between them. Over several meetings the growth group encouraged the intern to muster the courage to talk with his supervisor about the difficulties. It was also evident that the intern had projected onto his supervisor part of his own negative father complex, with its usual fear of persons in authority. Finally, the intern decided to make an appointment to speak to his supervisor.

After the intern had bravely told his pastor-supervisor his view of the difficulties between them, the supervisor replied that he would have to think these things over, pray about them, and would speak to the intern again within two weeks. Only a few days later the pastor called the intern into his study and announced that, "God has spoken to me in a dream and has told me to fire you!" The incredulous intern was fired on the spot!

This action by the supervising pastor meant that the intern would receive no credit for his semester's work, then almost completed. He would have to repeat the internship at another church, and arrange to support himself and his family for the additional unplanned months required to complete another semester of internship. It was a major psychological and financial blow to the intern and it placed a cloud over his career.

When I learned of these events, I immediately called the intern's supervising pastor and asked to speak with him about the dream. I hoped that together we could find some framework for the dream that would allow the intern to complete the semester. I thought that at least we could examine the content of the dream—perhaps there were other scenes that would modify the command to fire the intern. It was unclear whether it was indeed the "voice of God" that the pastor had heard in the dream, or if this was merely his interpretation.

The pastor refused to speak with me about the dream. The field instructor from Perkins also called the pastor, again with no result. It seems, therefore, that *the supervising pastor was unwilling to consider that God might not have spoken to him in a dream and told him to fire the intern*. He would not discuss the psychodynamic possibility that his own personality traits, or hidden conflict with the intern, rather than the voice of God, might have been represented in the dream.

Shortly after this incident, and at the end of the semester, Perkins held a general meeting which included myself, all the interns, the field instructor, and every supervising pastor but one. The pastor who had fired his intern refused to come to this meeting, at which the central topic of discussion was that very incident. There was nearly unanimous disapproval of the behavior of this pastor who refused to reconsider his dream and the action based on it. Many of his motives were discussed. Some even doubted that the supervising pastor had had a dream at all, and suggested that he had attributed his decision to a dream in order to avoid dealing directly with the intern about the conflict between them.

A second important point about this story is that *not one person at the semester meeting was willing to consider that God might actually have spoken to the pastor in the dream!* Here we have a vivid example of *both* sides of the current and crucial issue regarding the image of God in dreams. Do dreams sometimes have religious meaning, as the fundamentalist pastor alleged? Is it unthinkable that God might speak in a dream? The consensus of the discussion meeting seemed to be the latter.

These questions would not be raised by an orthodox Freudian, who doubtless would interpret an image of God as an image of the personal father, most likely the castrating father of the childhood oedipus complex. But in most religious traditions, for ages, there was no doubt that God *might* speak in a dream, although distinguishing whether it was God or mischievous spirits influencing the dream was always an issue.

The incident between the intern and his supervisor illustrates the stark contrast of these two positions for the present world. The pastor who fired his intern apparently did believe that God speaks in dreams, and God had spoken to him. The rest of the Perkins field unit, pastors and interns alike, seemed to take the position that God would never speak in a dream. Is there no middle ground between these positions? Is there no way to establish some common conversation between religious and clinical approaches to the meaning of dreams?

These events I have related involved either the excessive meaning or meaninglessness in dreams. They provided me with a major impetus to write a book about religious images, including the image of God, that appear in dreams.

It now seems appropriate to reflect at length upon the unconscious processes that affect the image of God in dreams. Even though such questions involve the deepest concerns of both religion and Jungian depth psychology, they are also indeed part of everyday clinical practice. Since the theories we hold influence not only our interpretations but also what we select for attention, an exploration of the images of the divine in dreams may be useful to others in the clinical practice of psycho-therapy and psychoanalysis, as well as in religious counseling. And perhaps it will stimulate some theological thinking.

Let me add a word about the term "God." I have used several forms in the text: "God," "god," and "god-image." One of the basic purposes of the discussion is to keep open the question of the metaphysical reality of "God" and the possibility that such a reality might reveal something of itself through symbols in dreams. Quotation marks (as in "God") imply a bracketing of the question of God, while the capitalized traditional form—God—gives more weight to the possible existence of a reality worthy of that name. I have also used "gods" and "god-image" in the usual manner of Jungian literature to refer to the many images of God in various mythologies and religious systems. From a purely psychological point of view, gods and god-images are personified archetypes.

In addition to those persons already mentioned, I wish to express my particular thanks to Perkins School of Theology for allowing me for so many years the privilege and pleasure of taking part in their intern program. Having spoken to pastors who entered their ministry years before the existence of anything like an intern program for ministers, I am deeply aware of how much strength and depth the Perkins program has added to the pastoral ministry.

I also wish to acknowledge the continuing stimulation and friendship of Frederick J. Streng, Professor of the History of Religions at SMU, whose knowledge of current Buddhist-Christian dialogue has kept alive my own interest in the relationship between the Jungian theory of dreams and the possibility of religious realities in the universe. Suzanne, my wife, deserves thanks for excellent advice and proofreading. Sherry Mize was helpful in preparation of the manuscript and Angela Lee was, as always, a necessary and appreciated support.

Thanks also go to Robert Moore and to Daniel Meckel for undertaking editorship of the series in which this volume appears, and for their encouragement, support, and advice.

I, of course, remain the plentiful and sole source for all error and confusion in these chapters.

James A. Hall
Dallas, January 1990

Introduction: Unconscious Christians

For several years I had in psychotherapeutic treatment a man who had at one time wanted to be a minister.[1] In fact, he had been quite serious about that career choice, feeling that he was "called" to it by God. His wife had supported him in whatever he wanted to do, but as time passed he let this sense of calling to the ministry slip away. He entered an entertainment career and became successful and financially stable. At the time that I saw him, he and his wife were separated. Both of them, however, seemed motivated to rehabilitate the marriage.

Chris (a pseudonym) and his wife were each in individual psychotherapy but attended the same group psychotherapy sessions, a format of treatment I have found quite useful for many couples. Although separated, they still spent one evening a week together and were sexually intimate. On another standing afternoon date, Chris met with his long-term paramour, a married woman. On other nights he frequently visited a well-known local bar and picked up women with whom he had casual sexual involvements. If Freud had been right about repressed sexual impulses being the cause of neurosis, Chris should have been neurosis-free, for clearly he was expressing his sexuality in an uninhibited manner.

In the midst of his frantic "sexual schedule," Chris had dreams with an unexpected theme. He dreamed of going to church and taking communion! What should we make of this? It was certainly not repressed sexuality that showed forth in Chris' dreams. I would suggest, rather, that it was his *repressed religious feeling!* While Chris' outer life had become entirely secular and quite hedonistic, his unconscious, the maker of his dreams, was vitally concerned to return to his life the missing religious feelings that had at one time been dominant. One could say that Chris was an *unconscious Christian.*

Is Chris a rare example, or do we find in many persons today a hidden religious impulse, one that has lost connection with the usual cultural forms of church and congregation? In current western society, many persons have abandoned conscious religious concerns. My experience suggests that these repressed, left-out religious feelings may return in dreams. It is important that this possibility be recognized and responded to by secular psychotherapists and religious counselors alike.

In my practice I have seen many persons whose religious concerns have gone "underground," into the unconscious, from which they return in dreams. These cases illustrate Jung's point that the natural function of a dream is to compensate for an unbalanced state of consciousness, and to return to the dreaming mind material that has been ignored by consciousness. Unconscious Christians such as Chris are not rare in our culture, and yet the repression of religious values is seldom acknowledged. This is partially because our culture still assumes a Freudian, corrective attitude toward the Victorian over-repression of sexuality in the name of religion. But, just as the Victorians were prudish about sex, we have become prudish about honest religious concerns. Too often religion is equated with strict and oppressive morality, particularly regarding sexuality. In some circles, religious behavior is still regarded as evidence of neurosis.

Jung believed that any person raised in western civilization has been deeply influenced, consciously or unconsciously, by the Judeo-Christian tradition. Thus many persons fit the description of an "unconscious Christian." They deal *un*consciously with religious problems and may have no conscious awareness of any religious conflict or concerns at all. Not all unconscious religious concern is Christian, but there are many Christians who are unconscious of their religion.

Repressed religious and moral concerns do not simply disappear. One of the basic findings of all depth psychology is that repressed contents reappear in consciousness, usually in projected, symbolic forms such as symptoms, confusions, and life-crises. Repressed religious concerns may also take such forms.

My area of expertise in depth psychology is Jung's *analytical psychology*, a unique system of theory, observation, and practice that Jung developed after he broke with Freud in the second decade of the twentieth century. Based on his inner life and his attempt to come to terms with the disturbing experience of breaking with Freud, Jung found his own ground by establishing his theory of the psyche and its functions. Terms like "introversion" and "extraversion," which have passed into common usage, were coined by Jung to describe differences in the way he, Freud, and Adler approached the psyche. Today there is a growing acquaintance with many other Jungian concepts.

Jung claimed that he never had a patient in the second half of life whose problem was not ultimately a "religious problem." By this Jung meant a crisis about deeper values and meaning. Furthermore, Jung declined to treat persons for whom traditional religious beliefs and practices seemed to carry sufficient meaning. If the archetypal symbols carried by the traditional religious images were effective in a person's life, Jung did not want them to embark on the long, arduous, and sometimes inconclusive search for a *personal* religious meaning. Traditional religious images and practices are like well-worn paths. They are suitable without question for many people. Psychologically, we might say that traditional religions are like umbrellas of symbolism which shield us from the too-bright light of direct perception of divinity, the archetypal experience attributed to Moses on Mount Sinai.

Jung's concept of the *Archetypal Self,* the deepest foundation of individuality, is of special importance to the discussion of dreams.[2] This notion engages issues of moral commitment and transgression. It also raises questions about the limitations of the human condition, and the horizons of human aspiration and inquiry. We will deal more fully with the concept of the Archetypal Self in the pages to come. In the classical Jungian view, it is directly related to the image of God in dreams and is the source of unconscious religious impulses.

Religion, especially the Christian tradition, was a lifelong concern of Jung's and influenced his psychology in ways yet to be thoroughly explored. Author Murray Stein has characterized Jung as a "physician of the soul," viewing Jung's work as an attempt to heal the ailing Christian tradition.[3] It is likely that Jung's psychology will influence evolving Christian understanding, particularly as it is experienced in practice by individuals.

In a dream, the individual may directly experience a symbolic image of the Archetypal Self, which Jung defines as an inner image of God. Jung is careful, however, not to assert that the Self is actually a representation of God in the psyche. He claims, rather, that one can find in dreams a range of similar images used by the psyche to indicate the Self and to represent the traditional meanings of God. We will henceforth call the Archetypal Self simply the "Self," using a capital "S" to distinguish it from ego concerns such as self-awareness, self-assurance, etc.

From an empirical point of view, the Self often appears clothed in the traditional imagery of God. This is because in Jungian theory the Self is the actual center of the psyche, while the ego is only the center of consciousness. Because the relationship of ego to Self is that of a specialized part to the whole, this relationship may be symbolized in a dream by images of a center and its periphery. In the older model of the atom, for example, the Self and the ego would be represented, respectively, by the nucleus and an orbiting electron. In political imagery, the Self may appear as the ruler of a political unit—a king, queen, president, or prime minister, for example. The ego, on the other hand, is often represented in a dream as an ordinary person. In a similar manner, when employing traditional religious imagery, the Self may appear in such images as Zeus, Jesus, Buddha, Siva, or some other central religious image of a culture.

Later we will deal with the intriguing fact that the image of God chosen by the dream will not always be drawn from the conscious religious tradition or concerns of the dreamer. This suggests that the unconscious dream-making function, attributed to the Self in Jungian theory, is committed to religious value, but not always in the same manner as the conscious ego personality.

Jung was always careful to distinguish psychological statements from theological statements. Throughout his writings, he claimed that he was not speaking metaphysically, but as an empirical psychiatrist, and that he was concerned only with *images* of God. He chose to leave questions about the metaphysical God to theologians and others who he felt had some special insight, as through revelation.

Yet, Jung's discovery of an organizing and stabilizing principle as the basis of the psyche—the Self—and its link to inner images of God, suggests an exciting approach to the exploration of religious phenomena. Though Jung did not assert it, his work clearly implies the belief that any theologian, even with the benefit of divine revelation, can speak of God and the images of God *only through the individual psyche*. This raises an important question which is the source of some tension in

Śiva, the Great Yogi.

The Archetypal Self is often represented in dreams by divine images from cultural settings that may or may not be familiar to the dreamer. In the dreams of Christian patients, the Self has appeared in such forms as the Hindu god Śiva, the Buddha, Jesus, and the Greek god Zeus.

Jung's work. Did Jung feel that the empirical images of "God" found in the psyche are images of a true, metaphysical God? During a now well-known BBC interview, Jung was asked the question, "Do you believe in God?" An elderly man at the time, Jung took a moment voicing his reply. "I don't believe," he said, "I know!" Was this arrogance on Jung's part? Did his response reflect some form of gnosticism, of which he was often accused? Or was Jung merely speaking of the *image* of God, as he had often done in his younger years?

It is my opinion that Jung came to believe that the Self was somehow related to the metaphysical and theological God. Jung came to this conclusion cautiously and carefully. However, Jung wrote the twenty volumes of his *Collected Works* primarily for scientific and cultured communities.[4] As a scientist and physician, he was careful to give empirical evidence for his insights, often by making comparisons of archetypal imagery throughout history. It was not until his autobiography, *Memories, Dreams, Reflections*, that Jung stepped outside his role as empiricist.[5] Written late in his life, this work was inspired by a series of dreams. In it, for the first time, Jung relates his personal experiences of the psyche.

In *Memories, Dreams, Reflections*, Jung describes the visions that he experienced during his recovery from a severe heart attack in 1944.[6] Jung's descriptions of these visions have a powerful impact on the reader. At night, he felt that he was in a "garden of pomegranates," a Kabbalistic image of the higher world. He envisioned attending "the marriage of Tiphareth and Malkuth," also Kabbalistic figures which represent, roughly, a form of God and the earth itself—not unlike the mystical marriage of Christ and his church.

In one vision, Jung felt he was leaving the earth and would soon learn the true meaning of his life and work, and join those with whom he truly belonged. But his physician, in the form of a priest of Asklepios, floated up to him and called him back to life. Like many who have had near-death experiences, Jung felt some resentment at being pulled back into the ordinary world, which he experienced as box-like and isolated.

Jung's illness marked a turning point in his life and work. In subsequent writings, he devoted much less attention to questions of clinical treatment, and focused instead upon archetypal themes. His *Answer to Job* came like a torrent when he began to write it.[7] He then wrote *Aion*, subtitled "Researches into the Phenomenology of the Self".[8] *Aion* forms the basis for our later discussion of the Self. Jung's final works include *Mysterium Coniunctionis*, one of the most difficult of his works[9]; his autobiography[10]; a few essays; and the editing of *Man and His Symbols*.[11]

In this remarkable outpouring of work in his later years, Jung sought for a way to describe his intuitions about the archetypal foundations of the human psyche. His diagrams in *Aion* are particularly important in that regard (see chapter 6). In the course of this volume, we will see how Jung's clinical theory of dream interpretation from his earlier clinical work may be combined with the intuitive images of the Self from this final period of his work.

Jung understood dreams to reflect a major dialogical process between two types of consciousness: the more limited and restricted world of ego-consciousness; and the wider, archetypal world of the "objective psyche"—Jung's later and preferred term for the *collective unconscious*. The objective psyche is outside the personal sphere and is considered more or less the same in all persons. This dialogue between the objective psyche and ego-consciousness is controlled by the Self, which Jung defined as both the totality of the psyche and its innate tendency toward order. Images of the Self may be indistinguishable from images of God, Jung states, although he never claims that God can be reduced to psychology. The most direct manner in which to view the Self is in dreams. Dreams are concerned with everyday events, but not exclusively so. Ultimately, they seem to focus on the process that Jung calls "individuation," the fulfillment in life of the innate possibilities of one's psyche.

Images of God appear in dreams in a variety of ways, along with many other religious images which originate in both Christian and non-Christian traditions. Jung believed that the *mandala,* for instance, is a religious image which commonly appears in dreams and represents the ordered Self. In this book, we will examine a number of religious images from dreams. In addition to clear and familiar images of God, we will encounter religious images that come from outside the dreamer's conscious experience, as well as images that appear to be religious only because of the context in which they are presented in the dream.

In looking at these images, we will examine the dream-making function itself and its relationship to humankind's innate concern with order, transcendence, and our best approximation of ultimate meaning.

In the chapters that follow, we will begin with a review of Jung's theory of dreams. This will serve as a backdrop to further discussion. Then we will look at some clinical examples of dream-images that directly or indirectly suggest the figure of God, and explore the relationship of these images to the Self. A clear understanding of this relationship can also help us to understand the problems which arise when the innate religious impulse is suppressed. Finally, we will raise the difficult question of empirical evidence for the Self, and ask what such evidence might mean for our theories of the psyche, as well as for clinical psychotherapy and for religious counseling.

Chapter 1

Interpreting Dreams: Jung's Theory

Jung's theory of dreams is the most important tool in the clinical application of his ideas about the psyche and psychopathology. In his earliest psychoanalytic writings, while still under the influence of Freud, Jung sometimes wrote as though he agreed with Freud's view that repressed sexual impulses form the basis of a dream's meaning. In this theory, the dream allows for a partial discharge of unacceptable and repressed impulses in disguised and symbolized form. This releases some of the original emotion that led to repression, but not enough to awaken the dreamer. The dream, in this early view of Freud's, is thus the "guardian of sleep."

Jung's break with Freud is the most significant schism in the history of psychoanalysis. After breaking away, Jung began to use his own fantasy and dream material to develop a new theory of the nature and function of the psyche and of dreams. He had as background not only his psychoanalytic experience with Freud, but also his early work with the word-association experiment at the Burgholzli Hospital in Zurich.[12] His interpretation of the word-association experiment, prior to Freud's influence, had led Jung to the notion of "emotionally-toned complexes." These complexes were, he believed, the basic patterns of the mind and were related to the imagery in dreams.

In short, a *complex* is a group of related images which are based upon an archetypal core and tend to have a common emotional tone. Any image associated with the complex may lead to a release of emotions. For example, a woman who has a negative

Sigmund Freud: Given by Freud to Jung in 1906.

Carl Jung, 1912.

father complex may find that negative feelings color her consciousness whenever she interacts with any male who evokes an image associated with the complex. Jung often finds it useful to consider the figures in dreams as personifications of the dreamer's complexes. There are also larger groups, or "fields," of complexes. These are organized into basic structures in the psyche, structures which he called the "shadow," the "persona," the "anima" and the "animus." Let us look briefly at each one of these concepts which are central to Jung's psychology.

The *shadow* is an alter-ego image. It contains complexes that have been dissociated from the ego and labeled "not-I." This occurs because of judgments, made during the early phases of personality development, about what is an acceptable self-image. The shadow is most often seen when it is projected onto another person, usually someone of the same sex. One may either admire this person, as in the case of a positive shadow projection, or dislike the person, in the case of negative shadow projection.

Most psychotherapeutic work consists of reworking the shadow by bringing it to consciousness and then reevaluating, by more mature standards, what is or is not acceptable for inclusion in the self-image. In dreams, the shadow may be symbolized in many ways. It may appear as someone of another race, a criminal, a Nazi, a communist, or any other person who is judged undesirable from the viewpoint of the dreamer's conscious self-image.

The *persona* is made up of the outer roles that a person plays in relationship to others and to society. It is a normal part of the personality, but may become pathological if it is substituted for a developed ego-personality, which is the "self" (with a lower case "s"). The persona may also be pathological if it is underdeveloped. In this case, the self has too little private space in its interactions with the world. Too much persona isolates one from others, while too little persona makes one excessively vulnerable, since every interaction is a crucial test of self-acceptance by others.

We often strive consciously for a particular persona. This can be done, for instance, by acquiring an advanced academic degree, the completion of which brings about many persona changes such as the prestigious title of "Doctor." In some instances, working on the persona is a way of contributing to the positive and healthy growth of one's self-image. To hide behind the persona, however, is regressive and can impede greatly upon individuation and the establishment of intimate relationships.

The *anima* is a field of female imagery in the mind of a man; the corresponding masculine imagery in a woman's mind is the *animus*. The notions of anima and animus have often been misunderstood, particularly in feminist writings. This is because Jung's descriptions of them are derived primarily from observations of his analysands. Many of these persons came from a traditional European culture, in which the societal roles of men and women were rather rigidly defined.

I have come to understand the anima and animus as performing an identical function in both men and women. Therefore, I will use the combined term "anima/animus" to avoid suggesting a basic distinction between them. The function of anima/animus is to enlarge the personal field of self-activity by bringing one into relationship with another person, or with an activity that is highly valued. What we call "falling in love" often entails the projection of the contrasexual image onto another person. Less frequently, the projection may be directed onto something other than a person, as for example, a political cause, a business, or even a pet. When the anima/animus functions in a positive way *inside* the personality, it appears in dreams and fantasy productions as a kind of guide to the soul, a "psychopomp" which leads the small self toward the greater Self.

Just as there are positive and negative forms of the shadow and the persona, there are also positive and negative forms of the anima/animus. In their negative forms, they function to isolate and protect the self from being pulled out of its habitual modes of behavior and understanding. In this way, the anima/animus can play a part in sustaining a neurosis.

Since the field of anima/animus is based upon distinctions between what is considered male or female, its content will shift with evolving cultural patterns of sex roles. The *function* of anima/animus will, however, remain unchanged. Just as one can rework the shadow, it is also possible to rework the anima/animus. Through analysis or reflection upon life experiences, one can develop a more subtle and discerning understanding of what is male and female in the personality.

When a complex is integrated to some extent into the self-image, it can be called an "identity structure." The shadow is an identity structure, as is the ego. In contrast, the persona and the anima/animus can be called "relational structures." This is because the persona helps one relate to the outer world, and the anima/animus relates one to the more intimate or internal world.

Complexes make up the contents of the *personal unconscious*. Each complex is based upon an archetypal patterning in the objective psyche. The original form of the psyche is the Self, which we will examine more closely in chapter 5. Recent theory suggests that in neonatal development the Self "deintegrates" from its original unity. It does this in order to form the various archetypal fields, which in turn organize subsequent experience into complexes based on those archetypal fields.[13] One should think of the archetypal fields and the complexes they generate as remaining always under the organizing influence of the Self, from which they were elaborated.

Dreams are a function of the Self. They reflect its influence and serve to compensate for one's conscious state. More

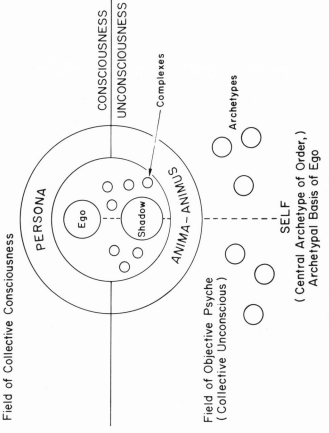

The Basic Structures of the Psyche.

specifically, they usually call into question one's conscious self-image. In the traditional Jungian view, this is done when the dream brings back to consciousness information and emphases that have been ignored or slighted by one's conscious attitudes. If, for example, one is excessively polite and subordinate in conscious relationships, a dream might compensate by showing one to be overbearing and aggressive. Dreams tend to compensate to the same degree that consciousness has become one-sided. If very little modification of the conscious position is indicated, a dream may make only a gentle correction which can even appear "complementary," rather than compensatory, to the conscious attitude.

Remembering dreams and reflecting upon them is itself a mode of compensation. The conscious awareness of potential meanings in a dream allows one to willfully create a balance in one's conscious views, and to further purify the self-image from neurotic thoughts and feelings that interfere with clear perception. In Jungian analysis, as the patient becomes aware of certain dream-images which are especially meaningful, these images often come to be referred to in a special "shorthand" language, shared by the analyst and patient. One might hear, for example, "That's your white rhinoceros again!"

Within the dream itself, there is yet another and more subtle form of compensation for imbalance in consciousness. This form does not rely upon formal analysis and seems to take place even when dreams are not remembered.[14] It is carried out in the action of the "ego-in-the-dream," which alters the structure of complexes upon which the waking-ego depends for its own view of itself and its world. This restructuring takes place in the dream, without the participation of the waking-ego.

In my clinical practice, I have come across many examples of this form. In one case, a man faced a basic father complex with which he had been identified for many years. His conscious knowledge of this complex had not been sufficient to free him from its compulsive influence. When the complex was faced in a dream, however, he seemed for the first time to achieve freedom from the action of the complex.[15] In another case, a woman who had spoiled several marriages because of a traumatic complex based on childhood experience was finally able to mitigate the action of the complex in her life after she directly dreamed of it.

This third form of compensation is found in addition to the traditional Jungian view of dreams. As I understand it, the Self "makes" a dream by structuring a dramatic situation based upon those complexes that are being worked on by the waking-self. Within that dramatic situation, the dream-ego finds that it is intimately involved in a drama that it did not create. This is why we may experience a dream as emerging *from* us, for it comes from the Self within us, but as not being *of* us, for we did not consciously choose which dream to have. As Cocteau once said, "The dreamer must accept his dream."[16]

The dream-ego works with personifications of the same complexes that compose, in part, the structure of the waking-self. Any changes in the structure of those complexes will therefore affect the personality experienced by the waking self. Changes are felt in the emotions particularly. We all have had the experience of feeling upset when we go to sleep, and waking up with a sense of renewal. Shakespeare noted how sleep (and dreams) can "knit up" the ravellings of the day. Most of us have also had the opposite experience of going to sleep feeling well and waking up feeling disturbed. In many instances it is possible to trace the disturbing emotion to a dream.

These experiences of being either "put together" or "taken apart" during sleep are familiar to almost everyone. I will give two examples which I have encountered. In the first, a woman went to sleep with a sense of uneasiness she could not explain. She awoke feeling that everything was all right. Then she remembered having a dream in which her mother, a compulsive housekeeper, had been scrubbing the dreamer's kitchen floor with an old brush and pail. The patient interrupted her, gave her tea, and told her that the maid was coming and would clean the kitchen floor with a new electric mopping machine. In the second example, a graduate student went to bed feeling secure and happy. He awoke with a start from a dream in which he was late for a final examination but had forgotten to go to class and did not know where the examination was to be. He took this anxiety dream as a comment on his recent laxity in study.

Jung's principle of compensation covers most clinical uses of dreams. But there is another important principle which Jung uses in interpreting dreams. It states that *the dream is a self-representation of the state of the psyche.* As we will see in the next chapter, this principal is crucial to understanding the meaning of images of God in dreams. For if it is correct, we can expect that dream-images of God will tell us about the very structure of the psyche. Moreover, if we consider the possibility that God, or any other religious reality, might actually influence dreams, then *the self-representation of the psyche in a dream may also represent a divine reality that works in us, in dreams, as well as outside us, in the world.*

Given this basic overview of the classic Jungian approach to dream interpretation, let us now look directly at some religious images and their meanings as they are found in dreams.

Chapter 2

Religious Images in Dreams

Throughout the history of most religious traditions, dreams have been considered as a source of information about the will of God and the existence of a spiritual world behind, above, or within the world of daily reality. Buddha's mother dreamed that a white elephant with many tusks entered her side—a foreshadowing of the birth of the historical Buddha. The ancient Greeks assumed that when a person slept within one of the Asklepian temples centered at Epidaurus, the god would send dreams to diagnose illness and indicate treatments. There were apparently many cures, attested by votive offerings of thanks at the shrines. The healing cult of Asklepios spread from Epidaurus in Greece to more than two hundred temples in the ancient world. It was perhaps the most highly institutionalized use of dream interpretation in history.[17]

In the Christian tradition, it was a dream that warned Joseph to take the infant Jesus and flee to Egypt to escape Herod's slaughter of the innocents. And a dream told him it was safe to return. In the Hebrew scriptures we find one of the oldest recorded examples of dream interpretation. Joseph, the son of Jacob, interprets two of Pharaoh's dreams and thereby foretells seven years of plenty followed by seven years of famine.[18] This is an example of the tendency in antiquity to see the dreams of a king as references to his kingdom, rather than as reflections of his personal life. The gospels do not record any of Jesus' dreams, but in the Buddhist texts we do find several of the Buddha's dreams.[19]

30

The conception of the Buddha. Maya, mother of the Buddha, dreams that an elephant descends into her womb.

Aesculapius (Greek: Asklepios). God of medicine and healing. In the Asklepian healing cults of ancient Greece, illness was diagnosed by interpreting dreams.

Dreams have had profound significance in the myths and histories of most world religions.

31

Joseph, the son of Jacob, interprets Pharaoh's dreams.

Many other traditions considered dreams an important source of knowledge not available in ordinary waking life. Homer believed that true dreams come through gates of horn; false dreams through gates of ivory. Virgil assigned true dreams to the hours before midnight. Dreams after midnight were potentially deceptive. Throughout the Middle Ages, dreams were accorded high status, yet one had to discern dreams sent by God from dreams sent by deceptive powers.

Today, dreams tend to be neglected in the practice of secular psychotherapy as well as in pastoral counseling. This is true despite their traditional importance in most religions, and the central role which the dream has played in the development of depth psychology. In Freud's early and influential works, dreams are nothing less than "the royal road to the unconscious." Yet, I believe that the current lack of interest in dreams is related to the limitations of Freud's dream theory, which until recently has been widely and tacitly accepted. According to Freud, the *manifest content* of a dream is the remembered dream specimen. What one remembers is simply a disguised version of the *latent content*, which represents an infantile wish, usually of a sexual or aggressive nature.[20]

In contrast, in the previous chapter we saw two ways in which Jung proposed that the meaning of dreams be understood. The first is that dreams operate according to a principle of compensation, by providing unconscious corrections for conscious imbalance or distortion. This notion is more complex that it may at first seem. Children's dreams, for instance, sometimes appear to compensate for problems in the family situation which are not simply those of the child. Some dreams and visions (waking dreams) in the history of scientific discovery have compensated for a lack of knowledge, not only in the dreamer but on the part of science as a whole. Kekule's discovery of the chemical form of benzene is a famous example of this. Struggling to unlock the chemical structure of the benzene mol-

The Uroboros, or tail biting serpent, is a symbol of eternity. It appears in ancient Egyptian papyri as well as in the earliest alchemical texts, such as the one pictured above. A dream image of an Uroboros led the 19th-century German chemist Kekule to discover the molecular structure of benzene—a ring.

ecule, he had a vision of a snake holding its tail in its mouth—an *uroboros*. From this vision, Kekule correctly deduced that the structure of benzene was in the form of a *ring*. Such instances suggest that dreams may at times help to provide knowledge of actual situations and point to the verifiable structure of reality. This "objective" approach to dream interpretation stands in contrast to Jung's second, "subjective" way of viewing dreams. Here the dream is understood as a self-representation of the state of the psyche. To thoroughly analyze a dream, one must consider both approaches. It is my own style always to consider the subjective approach first, but to remain mindful of the possible validity of an objective interpretation.

Some dreams do indeed seem to be self-representations of the human psyche through archetypal symbols. Because of this, we may expect to find images which are similar and yet derive from different cultures. Two of my own dreams made me acutely aware of this fact.[21] These dreams occurred during my first period of analysis, about two weeks apart. They were in some ways similar; but the second dream contained a striking archetypal image that I did not fully understand at the time. The first of the two dreams was as follows:

> Two young boys, about five years old, are living in the house in which I grew up. They wish to get out of the house. One is able to and one is not.

The second, archetypal dream occurred two weeks later. It had a similar structure:

> I am beside the same house, my childhood home. A large mother animal, somewhat like an elephant, has two small cubs about the size of dogs. I am my current age [at the time of the dream] and decide to take one of the cubs as a pet. As I pick up the cub, the mother animal becomes angry. She

seems to get larger and more agitated. Her left eye, the only
one that I can see, glows red with anger. I feel it best to
return the cub to her.

These two dreams have both significant parallels and
striking differences. The setting of each is my childhood home.
In the first dream, the two boys are inside the house, although
one of the boys gets away. This dream is seen from the point of
view of a spectator; the dream-ego is a floating "I" that does not
participate directly in the action. In the action of the second
dream, the dream-ego is clearly the protagonist. At first there
seems to be a direct parallel between the boys and the cubs. One
of the boys gets out of the house, and one of the cubs is to be
taken away as a pet. But this parallel is interrupted by the decision of the dream-ego to return the cub for fear of the mother's anger.

In recording this dream, I first wrote that this large, mater-
nal animal resembled an elephant. Then I corrected myself, for
the dream animal seemed too primitive to be an elephant, and
wrote that it was perhaps a mastodon. Still not satisfied with my
description, I finally recorded that it looked most like a tapir
enlarged to the size of an elephant—a giant tapir. My analyst at
that time was influenced largely by the psychology of Harry
Stack Sullivan. Appropriately, he interpreted both of my
dreams as referring to a positive mother imago and the problems associated with that family role. He did nothing specific
with the most striking image of the second dream—the large
animal. For over a year my dream report remained neatly patted
into the familiar interpretive form of a positive mother complex, associated with the *puer aternus*—"the eternal boy."

About a year later, I was living in another city and for a
time had not been in analysis. While casually reading an article
about the Cuña Indians of Central America, I made a startling
discovery.[22] One of their traditions concerned a *giant tapir!* Its

name was Achusimmutupalit, and I was amazed at how closely it paralleled my own dream. In Cuña Indian mythology, this giant tapir is believed to be the spirit of the Earth Mother's placenta. Its purpose is to keep plants, animals, and people from being picked off the tree of life—just as the giant tapir in my dream did not want me to remove one of the cubs! I had unexpectedly discovered a parallel between my dream and the mythology of the Cuña, not only in the image of the giant tapir, but also in its function. *Synchronicity*

I knew nothing about Cuña mythology. And yet my Self, in making the dream, somehow "knew" that the giant tapir was the right image to express something in my own psyche! There are several possible explanations for this. The most logical would be "cryptomnesia," an old psychiatric term which suggests that something once known but then forgotten may come back to consciousness as if from nowhere. Again, however, I am sure that I had read nothing about giant tapirs. A second explanation, one more popular today, is reincarnation. According to this belief, I may have been a Cuña in some past life. Some of the knowledge of that past life carried over into this one, and eventually became manifest in my dream.

A third explanation might assume some sort of extrasensory perception at an unconscious level. According to this theory, my unconscious reached out for information about the giant tapir from the mind of someone else by telepathy, perhaps from a living Cuña Indian or an anthropologist. Or, my mind might have used an unconscious clairvoyance—"seeing at a distance"—to learn of the material from a published source or archive.

Any of these theories might be invoked to explain the striking parallel between my dream-image and the image of the giant tapir in Cuña mythology. Personally, I find Jung's theory of archetypes most useful. One way of understanding the archetype is as a pattern of symbol formation which recurs

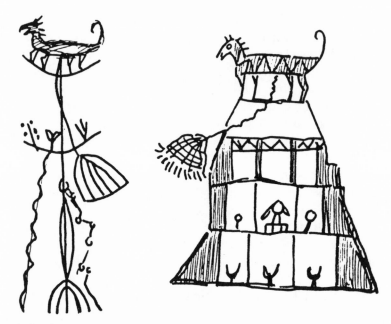

Achusimmutupalit, the placental dragon in Cuña Indian mythology, is said to be shaped like a tapir. Its purpose is to guard the Tree of Life (the placenta of the Great Earthmother) from which the original plants, animals, and humans are brought forth. The above line drawings of Achusimmutupalit were done by Cuña chief Ikwaniktipippi.

throughout human history. In our minds, we all have "fields" of such archetypes. At times, archetypal images appear in dreams and may strike us as both foreign and yet somehow appropriate. The archetypes themselves are present and, to some extent, are accessible to all human minds at a deeper level. One might even say that they somehow "live" in the objective psyche, for it seems that similar archetypal images carry a corresponding meaning in the dreams of different persons and, as we have just seen, in the mythologies of different cultures. This suggests their relative autonomy from the particulars of a given individual's life and his or her associations to a given dream.[23]

RELIGIOUS IMAGES THAT ARE FOREIGN TO THE CONSCIOUS LIFE OF THE DREAMER

The giant tapir in my dream belongs to the category of dream-images that have a religious meaning, but *not in the conscious associations of the dreamer*.[24] Consider the following striking example from my practice:[25]

A man in his mid-thirties suffered from an anxiety disorder so severe that he was confined to a radius of some seven blocks from his apartment. If ever he tried to go further, he would feel as though his heart were about to stop and that God was going to strike him dead. When intoxicated, he was able to go beyond the constricted radius in a car, so long as someone else was driving. His experiences with other therapists included treatment with drugs, as well as with electroconvulsive therapy. These treatments, incidentally, increased his radius of freedom by only a few blocks.

I saw him for two periods of one year each, but his symptoms were chronic and unimproved. Late one evening he called for an emergency appointment, claiming to be suicidal. His girlfriend had threatened to leave unless he improved and could take her to places outside his prison radius. I hospitalized him that evening and by the very next morning he was dramatically improved. Within two weeks he was driving himself, sober, on the loop around Dallas. He and his girlfriend were married soon thereafter.

I was astounded by his improvement! How, I wondered, did it occur so suddenly? Certainly it was not because of the medications he had begun only the night before. After much consideration, I decided that his startling improvement, after so many years of effort, was related to the following dream which he had the night of admission:

> I am a passenger on a boat going through a canal. The boat stops because a water monster is blocking the canal. Three young men dressed in loincloths and carrying spears are sent by the captain of the boat to remove the water monster. I am afraid they will be killed, but they are able to prod the monster out of the water. The boat then proceeds to move forward.

With no further information, I could easily relate this dream to my patient's clinical improvement. His anxiety problem (the monster) was removed by autonomous forces in his psyche (the captain and the three young men). His life (the progress of the boat) was about to resume. A new dimension of his dream was revealed, however, when I asked him to describe the water monster.

He described the monster as a large, hippopotamus-like animal with a strangely pointed head, and he later drew a crude picture of it. Remembering my own dream of the giant tapir, I hoped to find an archetypal amplification for this strange beast. The only hippopotamus figure that I was aware of in mythology or religious imagery was Ta-urt, the goddess of childbirth in ancient Egypt. However, while paging through a book on

Egyptian mythology, I stumbled upon another image that was an even more exact amplification. This was because the role of this mythic creature corresponded to the patient's fear of his heart stopping and of God striking him dead.

The image was not only that of a hippopotamus; it had the body of a hippopotamus *and* a pointed head (just like the monster in the dream). It was a monster pictured in the Papyrus of Hunifer: a hippopotamus with lion forepaws and the long and pointed head of a crocodile. The scene in which it appears is the judgment of the dead soul by the god Anubis. The judgment itself is pictured as the weighing of the heart of the deceased against the feather of truth, representing the goddess Maat. Should Anubis find that the heart fails the judgment against the feather of truth, it is tossed to this hippopotamus monster, who totally consumes it. This constitutes the final death of the soul.

The dreamer had no associations to the monster and no knowledge of having ever read Egyptian mythology. Nevertheless, the mythological role of this image was appropriate to the patient's personal symptoms. It represented the terror of his heart stopping (eaten by the monster in the mythological scheme) because God might strike him dead (Anubis judging the soul to be unworthy).

My experiences with this patient's dream and with my own dream of the giant tapir have further convinced me of the value of Jung's theory of archetypes. Without the notion of archetypes and archetypal images, one can explain these experiences only by evoking less adequate theories, such as those mentioned above.

The following is another example of a non-Christian image appearing in a Christian's dream. A man in his mid-thirties had a rather withdrawn social life and was trying to decide whether to become a psychotherapist (which he equated with being in contact with other people) or a laboratory researcher (which he equated with burying oneself in books).

The Egyptian Hippopotamus goddess Ta-urt, patroness of pregnancy and childbirth.

From the Papyrus of Hunifer: Anubis weighs the heart of the deceased against the feather of truth, while Ammit, the demon devourer of the dead, awaits the outcome.

While caught in this decision process, he dreamed the following:

> I am at dockside and I see an old girlfriend on board a ship about to embark. Anxious to see her, I rush up the gangplank, only to be suddenly stopped by a male figure, who says, "*If* you insist, maybe next time." I realize that all the people on the boat are dead.

The dream suggested that a part of him was anxious to pursue something from the (dead) past. Another internal force (the guard on the gangplank) was preventing him, but would cease to do so if he insisted. His realization that all the people on the boat are dead touches upon a very old archetypal theme: death as a journey across a river or a sea. At Luxor in old Egypt, the city of the living was on the east bank of the Nile, while the necropolis of the Valley of the Kings was on the west bank, the bank of the setting sun. In Greek mythology, death entailed crossing the river Styx. In Nordic culture, when a Viking chieftain died, his body was sent out to sea on his own burning ship. Some Christian imagery suggests that death entails a water passage, though it is most often thought of as a movement from the earth up to heaven, or down to hell. While this patient was consciously a Christian, the imagery of his dream seemed to reflect other, non-Christian traditions. I have seen many such images in the dreams of practicing Christian patients: images of the Buddha, the Hindu god Śiva, corn-god figures from American Indian mythology, the Kabbalistic Tree of Life, and several deities of Aztec derivation. It is likely that such religious images, unknown to the conscious mind of the dreamer, occur much more often than is generally realized. The analyst must, therefore, have some knowledge of comparative mythology to recognize such images.

How should we interpret the appearance in dreams of di-

Death is often depicted as a journey by boat. Above: From Greek mythology, Charon ferries a naked soul across the river Styx.

vine images which are foreign to the dreamer? I would hold that such appearances suggest that there is an unconscious religious impulse in the human psyche, and that this impulse is not concerned with one's conscious tradition. This innate religious function in the psyche is spiritual to be sure, but is neither denominational nor dogmatic.[26]

IMAGES FROM THE DREAMER'S RELIGIOUS TRADITION

In my experience, the largest number of religious images in dreams stem from the dreamer's own tradition. Traditional religious images often appear in a form consistent with their meaning in the conscious religious beliefs of the dreamer.

A curious subcategory consists of religious dream-images that manifest themselves in a manner not entirely consistent with their usual meaning. This phenomenon again reflects the autonomy of the unconscious in its use of religious images. The patient who dreamed of the embarking ship reported another dream of this latter type. In this dream, the symbol of crucifixion is used in an unusual manner, but which is still congruent with the traditional meaning of the instrument of death preceding resurrection:

> I am waiting in line to be crucified. I am terrified when my younger brother approaches me and says, "Look at the nail holes in my hands! I've been through this and it's not so bad!"

This dreamer had remained single and was somewhat shy in dating women, whereas his younger brother had married successfully and had a child. He understood the dream to mean that his younger brother had already been through the problems of a relationship, which the dreamer had avoided as if they would be "crucifyingly" painful. He felt that the meaning of his waiting in line to be crucified in the dream indicated a complete cycle of death *and* resurrection/transformation.

Because of the relative timelessness of the unconscious, the sequence of dreams is not as crucial as the sequence of consciously recorded events. The same structure of complexes can be returned to again and again in a series of dreams, seen once from one point of view, again from another. Moreover, any particular complex may be represented by many diverse images. Thus, it is possible to put together two other dreams of this young man; dreams which would, in ordinary dramatic sequence, have come in reverse order.

Here is the first dream:

> I am talking to an unknown young man about his dreams. One of the dreams is of Christ. In his dream, Christ tells him that he has tickets for the man and three other men to fly on an airplane to an important destination. Christ indicates that he himself will direct the flight. The young man also tells me that both Christ and the number four can symbolize the Self or Central Archetype in Jungian dream theory, and that the dream sounds propitious for a movement toward individuation.

While recounting this dream of Christ within his dream, the patient recalled a second and earlier dream in which he had to pilot an airplane unfamiliar to him. A mysterious ground controller, however, was giving him instructions by radio as to how to fly the plane, and thus he felt safe. *If* the second dream had preceded the first, and *if* the dream of Christ had occurred directly to the dreamer, instead of being reported by another figure in his dream, the two dreams together would suggest a promise by Christ to direct the flight. It would also indicate the fulfillment of the promise by the mysterious ground controller, probably another image of the Christ figure.

The man who had these religious dreams is from a traditional religious family background, but it is clear that his dreams used religious imagery in a non-traditional manner. His other dreams included one in which he "observed the crucifixion of St. Peter," and an initial dream in which "Hamlet and Christ were approaching each other slowly and when they met, a huge explosion was going to occur." Some of his dreams were more subtle, with the traditional religious image occurring only with amplification, as in the dream that "there was a heavy log on my back, with thorns on it, but someone helped to lift it off, and I felt better." His associations suggested Christ carrying his own cross to Golgotha, perhaps also combined with imagery of the crown of thorns, in the dramatic sequence of the Stations of the Cross.

This man is another example of an "unconscious Christian." In his waking life he was not especially concerned with religious or moral questions. Like the patient who was engaged in excessive sexual pursuits and yet dreamed of taking communion, the life of religious and spiritual concern had fallen into his unconscious. It became evident only through his dreams.

Another group of dream-images that fall under this general category includes traditional religious images containing secular meanings. This type is rare, however. Such a dream occurred in the life of a woman patient who, as it became clear in the course of therapy, was uncomfortable about her sexual identity, although she had been heterosexually active. In her dreams, male animus figures were often represented by men she knew, in waking life, to be either homosexual or bisexual. In structural terms, the sexual identity of her self-image and that of her animus were poorly differentiated. At a point of improvement in therapy she had this dream:

Christ is on the cross, but instead of being in agony he has an erection and is saying, "Heaven help us, I'm not asbestos."

She associated this last phrase with a Fred Astaire movie. The song, "I Won't Dance," speaks of a person who refuses to dance for fear of being overcome with passion. This imagery helped to compensate for her avoidance of relationships for fear of being overwhelmed, although she consciously desired connection with others.

CONGRUENT RELIGIOUS IMAGES FROM DIVERSE CULTURAL TRADITIONS

The following is an unusually clear example of how a dream may employ religious images from different cultures. It suggests that the psyche is aware of these different archetypal images and focuses more upon the effect of the religious image than its intelligibility is to the conscious ego. The female patient just mentioned had encountered severe problems in her relationship with her mother while growing up. After many years of both individual and group psychotherapy, she was able to overcome a strong negative mother complex, but it was impossible to work out a stable and loving relationship with her actual mother. The following dream occurred early in her analysis.

I am at the estate of my grandfather, looking at the swimming pool behind the house. On the floor of the pool is carved the face of Diana. A voice says to me, "You should see the statue of Diana at Ephesus!" The scene then quickly changes. In the second scene, I am on the ground floor of a two-story shack. The Virgin Mary is crying in the room above me. As the tears of the Virgin pass through the ceiling, they turn to blood, forming a pool on the floor of the room in which I am standing. I dip my hands into the pool of blood and am then able to see the spirit of my dead husband. We walk together and talk. He tells me that although I want to be with him, I must stay on earth to raise our children.

Notice the striking concurrence of a carved image of the Roman goddess Diana and a living dream representation of the Virgin Mary. In Christian iconography, the Virgin has a rather stable meaning. She is always the helpful and comforting woman, whether in the story of her as the "handmaiden of the Lord" at the annunciation, or as the mother of sorrows at Christ's descent from the cross. In contrast, Diana exhibits a much wider range of meanings. She is the huntress and the goddess of the moon. In some forms she is close to the Virgin. Both Diana and Mary can be seen as forms of the Great Mother. Mary represents the Great Mother in the role of "Queen of Heaven" or "Mother of God." Diana conveys this meaning as the earth mother, particularly in her representation as Diana of Ephesus, the "Lady of the Beasts," with a multitude of breasts, symbolizing her ability to nourish all living things.

This dream was one of several, plus one waking vision, that seemed to provide this woman with a sense of the nurturing aspect of the mother archetype, which had been inadequately evoked by her experience of her personal mother. This case is an example of how, from the classic Jungian point of view, personal parents may restrict the expression of the original parental images rather than help represent their entire content. If the personal mother is the "carrier" of archetypal potentials, some of these potentials will be carried well, and others poorly or not at all. Consequently, the infant or child may experience the image of the personal mother as having the numinosity of

Virgin Mary, holding the Christ Child.

Diana of Ephesus, the many breasted mother goddess of fertility and fruitfulness.

the archetypal mother, while many of the archetypal potentials may remain in the unconscious, seeking other pathways of expression and influence in the child's developing consciousness, such as through dreams.

In the above dream, the Virgin Mary is portrayed in her traditional role as the mother of sorrows, which is consistent with her other roles in the Christian tradition. When the image of Diana appears in the bottom of the pool, however, a wide range of meanings could be inferred—from the angry and vengeful goddess (as in the myth of Actaeon, in which she is discovered nude in her bath) to the multibreasted form of the Great Mother. The authoritative voice from nowhere narrows the meaning by saying, "You should see the statue of Diana at Ephesus," the Diana with many breasts.

Now, the dreamer had no conscious knowledge of Diana of Ephesus. But some time after working with the dream, she recalled having read, years before, a book about St. Paul in which she believed there might have been a picture of a cult statue of Diana. It was probably correct that she had seen such a picture, because in the book of Acts, chapter 19, it is clear that Paul had a confrontation with the Ephesians and must have been aware of the temple of Diana in Ephesus. In fact, Ephesus is the traditional site of the Virgin's burial (although current dogma has her falling into sleep—*dormition*—and being taken into heaven). This association of Ephesus with both Mary and with the Great Mother role of Diana suggests that the similarities between these two goddess-images have occurred to many persons long before our present dreamer.

There are other archetypal images in her dream: that of a blood sacrifice in order to see and converse with the spirits of the dead, for example. But the central thrust of the dream, for our present purposes, lies in the double imaging of the Great Mother. The image of Mary is familiar and comforting. The image of Diana is far from conscious awareness, and yet its appearance in the dream gives greater emphasis to the caring aspect of the mother archetype. This emphasis is given by the dream-making Self, without apparent concern that the waking-ego understand the Diana imagery.

SECULAR IMAGES WITH RELIGIOUS MEANING

The difficulties in interpreting the image of God, and other religious images in dreams, are compounded by the fact that the psyche is able to attach religious meanings to virtually any image. Jung said frequently that the Self could appear in imagery traditionally associated with God. Yet Jung also said that *anything* can be an image of the Self, depending upon the context in which it is used. For example, he mentioned that snakes, elephants, and even spiders may represent the Self. Any image, religious or secular, which represents the whole as opposed to the disorganized parts tends to be an image of the Self and is, if we follow Jung's reasoning, equal in meaning to images of God. There are three forms of imagery that are often taken to represent wholeness. These are the mandala, the image of androgyny, and images of good fused with bad into a complete whole.

A mandala is generally a fourfold structure depicting peripheral forms with a central form of higher value. Although the mandala is a traditional image used for meditation in Tantric Buddhism, Jung discovered similarly ordered images in the dreams and fantasy material of his patients. The mandala symbolism most often occurred when a conscious self-image was disorganized and required strong compensation from the unconscious. For example, a man had this dream:

Mandala symbolism occurs in nearly all cultures, but is most commonly associated with Tibetan Buddhism, in which it is used for the practice of meditation. Mandalas often appear in dreams and fantasies as symbols of the Self, to compensate for a lack of integration and direction in one's waking life. Above: Mandala of the fivefold Buddha Shakyamuni.

> I see twelve divers with hoses radiating from a central hose; they are exploring different areas of the sea, but each always comes back to a large central rock jutting above the waves.

At another time the same dreamer reported:

> I am at a dam back home looking at a pool of water beneath the dam; I see a large creature with many radial legs.

He also dreamed of a small black triangle inside a larger triangle. The name of the small triangle was "Alto," which he associated with "the highest female voice and the lowest male voice—a unification of the opposites."

All of these mandala-like images of higher order seemed to compensate for the lack of order and direction in this man's conscious life. As he became more oriented toward his own individuation, the frequency of such images of order decreased.

Another man dreamed:

> I am about to feed a strip of roast beef to a small turtle on the floor when the turtle suddenly rises high above the floor and takes the entire strip of meat in one bite, barely missing my fingers. I realize it isn't just a turtle; it is also somehow a dragon.

Only years later did the dreamer discover an Oriental image of a "dragon-turtle," said to be a combination of masculine sky forces (dragon) and feminine earth forces (turtle), and therefore an image of totality.

THE UNIFICATION OF OPPOSITES AS A RELIGIOUS SYMBOL

Because the Self appears also as the image of God, I have included dream images of the unification of opposites as another category of religious images in dreams. Jung encountered images of the unification of opposites in both clinical dream material and in medieval alchemical writings. In *Mysterium Coniunctionis*, his last major work, Jung dealt with the "coniunctio," an alchemical term for the unification of opposites.[27] This union was the primary operation of alchemy, for which all other operations were merely preparatory. The coniunctio represented the final creation of the alchemical *lapis*, the philosopher's stone, a strange substance that could allegedly transmute gross metals such as lead into pure gold. "The alchemist's statements about the lapis, considered psychologically, describe the archetype of the self," wrote Jung.

I recall one seemingly ordinary and brief dream that contained a whopping dose of alchemical imagery. A young man dreamed:

> I am watching a pot of percolating coffee. As it keeps recycling, the coffee is turning into gold.

Here, in one short dream, are the alchemical motifs of *circulatio* (the repeated circulation of the dark substance), *nigredo* (the black substance), and, of course, the making of gold! In another example of the union of opposites, a man dreamed that he was in bed with a very attractive young woman. However, when he began to be sexually intimate with her, he discovered that she had a small penis as well as a vagina. He felt that in waking life this would repulse him. Yet in the dream it indicated to him that she was complete in herself and did not need him (it was not clear whether or not she would relate to him sexually). The *androgyne* is an ancient symbol of wholeness, in which male and female are united in one body. One example is the Hindu god Śiva, who is sometimes depicted in androgynous form as *Ardhanarisvara*, "The Lord whose Half is Woman."

An alchemist kneels in prayer in a laboratory cell amidst his various alchemical instruments.

Ardhanarisvara: The Lord whose Half is Woman. In this androgynous manifestation, Śiva and his consort Parvati are united as one being.

The most complete image of the unification of opposites which I have encountered was in a dream which reads like a fairy tale. The dreamer, a middle-aged woman, was caught in a situation in her marriage which greatly troubled her. Essentially, she felt a strong love for her husband, but this love was combined with strong moral disapproval. She dreamed:

> I am the wife of the good king. Our daughter, the princess, has just married and is spending her wedding night on the train where we live. My husband, the good king, is with his ministers who are urging him not to fight the bad king again until his wounds are healed from their last encounter.

In this opening movement of the dream we have at once the opposing figures of a "good" king and a "bad" king. They represent, in personified form, the basic moral tensions in her life.

> My husband, the good king, says that he must fight the bad king right away. It is a point of honor.

Here we see the "downside" of being a good king. One must put honor above life, above letting the wounds heal. The dream-ego next sees the action from a detached point of view, as if it were floating above the scene rather than being a participant within it.

> I watch him ride out into the desert beside the train to meet the bad king for combat. The good king tells the bad king that he thinks there is some good in him, despite everyone thinking he is only bad.

This is the first statement which suggests that there may be some similarity in the two opposites; that they are not irreconcilably opposed. The good king presses the point further:

Since he is already wounded, the good king states that he will probably die in their coming battle. He asks the bad king to promise that if he, the good king, is killed in their battle, the bad king will take care of his widowed queen and his orphaned children.

His request draws an intense reaction from the bad king:

The bad king is so emotionally touched by the fact that anyone might believe there is some good in him that he bursts into tears.

Here is a further indicator that the "bad" king does not like his condition, but secretly wants to be seen as also "good." Next comes the most surprising moment in the dream:

While the bad king is blinded by his tears, the good king kills him!

The "good" king has used a psychological trick on the bad king:

Then the good king, having become not-so-good, rides back to the train. I, the queen, then find myself on the train again. I walk to the back of the train, further than I have ever gone before. There I find, to my great surprise, that the bad king had a compartment on that same train, where I live. In the bed of the deceased bad king, I find a small white kitten.

She concludes:

The bad king could not have been as bad as everyone said, or he would not have cared for this helpless white kitten. I pick up the kitten and carry it forward on the train so that I can give it to my daughter, the princess, to raise.

In this remarkable dream, we see most of the motifs found
in traditional fairy tales. Marie-Louise von Franz has shown
that such tales symbolize the patterns of ego development.[28]
These patterns entail the question of good and evil (which dif-
ferentiates the ego-image and the persona from the shadow);
the question of masculine and feminine relationship (the king
and the queen); and the transpersonal question of how stability
can be carried forward into the next generation of the "kingdom," symbolized by the marriage (the *coniunctio* archetype) of
the prince and princess. The white kitten (the "good" content
of the "bad" king) is carried forward to become part of the next
"generation" of the psyche.

In the life of the dreamer herself, this dream of the two
kings was the beginning of a change in conscious self-structure.
The woman found herself less judgmental and more able to
understand the meaning of her situation in a variety of ways.
She was moving away from the dogmatism of a strong ego/
shadow split, toward an increasing sense of compassionate understanding of herself and others. Jung discusses a dream very
similar to this good king/bad king dream in *Mysterium Coniunctionis.* He calls it "the dream of the black and white
magicians," both of whom were needed to accomplish the in-
tended task.

Some time later, my patient, who had been corrected in her
dogmatic religious stance by the good/bad king dream, received
yet another corrective dream from her unconscious. She had
become affiliated with a charismatic fundamentalist group, even
though she herself did not share the rigid moralistic framework
of her minister and many of her fellow church members. Instead, she found great meaning in some phenomena of the
"spirit": glossolalia and healing. At a time when she was moving
back in the direction of the black and white moralism which had
been interrupted by the good/bad king dream, she dreamed that
she and others were ascending a beautiful staircase to heaven.

Lovely music filled the air, as in the Hollywood musicals of the 1940s, which she loved. She had the sense of moving closer and closer toward heaven and of wonderful anticipation of meeting God. But as she neared the top of the stairs, she found that there was no heaven there at all. In fact, several ministers were "assisting" people at the top of the stairway by actually hurling them off into space! She awoke with a start.

It did not require symbolic interpretation for her to realize the warning of the dream, and once more she backed away from the judgmental side of her shadow, while continuing to enjoy its charismatic gifts.

We have now explored several ways in which divine images may appear in the dreams of ordinary persons living in contemporary western society. These explorations are not exhaustive, of course, and other images and categories could be included, such as dreams of "emptiness," which have a Buddhist flavor (see chapter 4). The examples which have been given here constitute only a sampling of the variety of religious images ordinarily found in dreams.

Do such images in dreams tell us only about the nature of the psyche? Or, do they show us the influence of a metaphysically "real" deity upon the human psyche? Perhaps this influence may even be seen *most clearly* in dreams. It is this last possibility which makes the examination of images of God in dreams especially exciting. In spite of all the metaphysical, theological, and psychological pitfalls of approaching dreams in this way, it does, however, seem possible that we might learn something about the nature of God from divine images in dreams. This may be true even though these images appear in ways that are both familiar and unfamiliar to us and to our conscious traditions.

Chapter 3

The Mysterious Symbolism of Dreams

Dreams are more profound and mysterious than we usually imagine them to be. Yet they are also familiar, on the "near side" of our experience. We thus tend to dismiss them as "only dreams," although we sometimes allow their images to frighten or inspire us. The latter is true especially when these images have a religious quality. No one can doubt that religious images appear in dreams. But how are we to understand the ultimate significance of these images? Do they reflect a real divine presence, or should we simply say that some experiences in life are best symbolized by God, Christ, Buddha, Śiva, the Virgin crying, or a giant tapir guarding her cubs?

It may well be that we shall never know with certainty the ultimate status of our dream-images, especially those that are religious.[29] And yet, even if we cannot see behind their appearances, the type of God-images and the manner in which they are used in a dream may clearly tell us something about the way the psyche experiences God. Whether or not these images tell us anything about a metaphysical God—the God of the theologians—is an intriguing matter which I, like Jung, am not qualified to explore in depth. However, if theologians (who also dream) wish to discuss the *image* of God in dreams, this is another matter indeed.

There are countless contemporary approaches to the interpretation of dream-images. Depending on the approach taken, the image of God in dreams will have very different meanings. Freud's theory is one of the best known, yet I find it hard to believe that dreams are merely symbolic masks of thoughts and feelings that are unacceptable to consciousness and therefore must be disguised in order to prevent the interruption of sleep. After all, many people dream of "unacceptable" things, such as sexual congress with a parent—things that Freudian theory says must be kept out of dreaming consciousness at all cost. Even Julius Caesar is said to have dreamed of sexual intercourse with his mother the night before he crossed the river Rubicon and changed the course of western history. Caesar's non-Freudian dream interpreter equated his mother with Rome, the mother country, and advised that if he marched on Rome she would receive him.

Certain other approaches to dreams also seem to me unreasonable or meaningless. They include many of the reductionist theories of sleep and dream researchers. The latter tend, in a supposedly "scientific" manner, to reduce the vast and complex tapestry of meaning in dreams to the mere neurological effects of discharges in the rostral pons of the brain stem. I also find it impossible to even consider many of the popular approaches to dreams, such as those which allow one to ask, "What should I do?" before going to sleep, and then expect that a dream will provide the answer! Dreams are profound and mysterious, and cannot be called on like an information service for answers to everyday questions. Otherwise, there would be many more millionaires and happy stockbrokers than exist today!

Like Freud, Jung, and many others, I do believe that the dream-image is *symbolic*. When Jung talked about a symbol, he meant something other than simply an image that, by convention, stands for something else (as a red traffic light stands for "stop"). Something that can stand in clearly for something else is what Jung called a "sign." Jung reserved the term "symbol" for something inherently mysterious. According to him, a symbol represents a reality that cannot, at that given time, be more clearly described. From this classic Jungian point of view, symbols have depth—unfathomable depth. It is true that the images in a dream may personify a psychological complex. But complexes and their related groups of images are themselves based upon archetypal cores which in turn are coordinated by the Self, the most mysterious of all Jungian concepts.

Again, a dream-image is a symbolic form "chosen" by the Self to express a reality that cannot, at that moment, be more fully understood. A symbolic image may refer to the past of the dreamer, even to unresolved past conflicts, particularly those related to self-image questions. It also may refer to current life circumstances, or to the need to find answers to one's questions about the nature of the world.

If, however, we take the "referent" of a dream-symbol to be the psyche itself, we are led straightaway to explore what are indeed the most enigmatic dimensions of life. For at its depths, the psyche is a realm about which, if we are open at all to metaphysical questions, we must admit that we know next to nothing. The anomalies of the psyche, such as those studied by parapsychology, suggest that the universe is a much more mysterious place than we ever dreamed it to be.[30] To approach the dream as referring to the psyche itself raises many issues, including the question of "precognitive dreams."

PRECOGNITION AND LIFE AFTER DEATH

Precognitive dreams indicate that the psyche has foreknowledge far beyond our waking selves. If such dreams really do occur, then we must consider that the unconscious, from which dreams arise, has a different relation to time than we experience in ordinary consciousness. In usual conscious life, the experience of time is inescapable. However much we may prefer to hold onto a present experience, the flow of time moves steadily onward, and what is present and real to our senses moves inexorably into the past and dissolution. This continual dissolution of the present can create in us a sense of the impermanence of all things—a sense which inspired the central insights of Buddhist thought. The Christian vision answers to this experience with the kingdom of Heaven, a permanent place that is immune to decay and change. At the bedrock of western philosophy, Plato envisioned a world of ideal forms, "in the heavens," that are eternal and unchanging, while what we see as "reality" consists of mere shadows on earth of these everlasting forms.

Precognitive dreams suggest that the Self, as the maker of dreams, is independent of time and thus vastly different from the waking-ego, the everyday self. What is a time-bound process to the ego may simply be "present" to the Self, although it is difficult to imagine what "present" means to a point of view outside of time as we know it. Being outside of time is not equivalent to being eternal, rather it resembles the state of the gods of mythology: beings relatively eternal and all-powerful in comparison to the brief lives and limited powers of humankind.

Perhaps the most provocative precognitive dreams are those which concern death—the most overaching problem in the strange process of being human. I would like to present two dreams concerned with death. I have chosen them as examples because, within each dream itself, the significance of the death-image is addressed. These dreams show, therefore, how the psyche itself speaks of death.

In his autobiographical volume, *Memories, Dreams, Reflections,* Jung recounts his dream of his wife Emma a year after her death.[31] In his dream, she appears on a stage; yet he knows that this is not Emma herself. Instead it is some kind of three-dimensional "portrait" that she has commissioned in order to show him, by means of the dream, that she is safe and secure, and that he need not worry about her. This dream-image is understood within Jung's dream itself, then, as having been constructed by what some parapsychologists would call a "discarnate personal agency," or in common language, the surviving soul of the deceased.

If dreams point to a reality that cannot be more clearly symbolized at the present time, perhaps Jung's dream points to a reality that has been affirmed for millennia by religious traditions of a vast number of cultures—the survival of the soul. Is it possible that Jung's dream-image of his wife Emma was indeed an inner reference to a postmortem reality? Evidence for such a belief might be found by looking for similar dreams, reported by other persons.

In my own practice, I have encountered such a dream. It was reported to me by a physician, the son of a medical missionary, within three months of his father's death.

> I see my father. His image speaks and says that it is not, in reality, my actual father. Rather, it is an existing image of the father, used by another consciousness, a messenger, to communicate to me that my actual father is safe [like Emma], but "far away" and unable himself to communicate at this time. My father is said to be at peace, a welcome contrast to his troubled and turbulent life.

What conclusions are we to draw from Jung's dream of Emma, the physician's dream of his missionary father, and many other such dreams? It is entirely possible, in the light of Jungian dream theory, that these dreams indicate an actual after-death survival of the deceased personality, which uses an ability to influence the dream imagery of the living (at least of those close to them in life) in order to convey a reassurance about the continuation of life beyond the death of the physical body.

The survival after death is an age-old archetypal theme in the history of humankind, and I cannot possibly give adequate treatment to it here. Any good orthodox Jungian would expect this theme to occur as an archetypal image even if there were no actual survival. We all, of course, will ultimately conduct our own "experiment" in surviving death. None, or at most very few, will return to tell us with any certainty of a "beyond." If the dead survive, they likely place little value in telling us about it. And yet we, the living, place great value in knowing if the human personality, or a significant part of it, survives physical death. To live with the belief of final annihilation, though it may be noble, is certainly different than living as though life will go on indefinitely into the future, even in altered form.

One of the most useful explorations of the meaning of death in relation to dreams is Marie-Louise von Franz's *On Dreams and Death.*[32] In her usual scholarly and incisive manner, von Franz probes the images of death in culture and in dreams. The book must be read in its entirety, but one of the dreams she cites has stayed vivid in my mind.[33]

A woman was dying and knew this fact. She was very frightened of death until only a few hours before her actual physical death, when she awoke from a brief sleep. She reported a dream to her nurse and a few hours later died peacefully. This dream seemed to alter her life profoundly, although she had only a few remaining hours. She dreamed that a candle was burning in the window of her room. As it burned lower and began to flicker, she realized that she would die when it went out entirely, and she was afraid. The candle sputtered and went out. For a moment there was complete darkness; but then the candle was burning again, *on the outside of the window pane!*

If the flickering candle symbolized the fading organic life of her body, what was symbolized by the re-lit candle on the outside of the clear window pane? Who can say? Perhaps the candle's flame was a symbol of the essence of life, continuing "outside," in a space which is not bounded like the room. Was this dream a mere compensation for the conscious fear of dying? Or was it perhaps a self-representation of the state of the psyche: the psyche that may "know" more than consciousness? Perhaps the psyche has experienced death repeatedly and sees it not only as an end but as a transition.

Whatever it reveals about the state of the psyche, the candle dream did what dreams at their best are supposed to do: it prepared the woman's ego for the next stage of life. In this case the next stage was death—the end of life as we know it consciously. The dream allowed her to live fully and actively right to the end, rather than being dragged to her death by the inexorable decline of her physical body.

The "what" and "why" of images in our dreams cannot be settled with any certainty. My own view is based upon intuitions ranging over a vast number of dreams from a wide array of patients over several decades of practice as a Jungian analyst. I believe that images in dreams are clearly symbols, not signs, and that they point to a deeper reality than that of the everyday world in which we live our lives. As the two "message" dreams discussed above suggest, the psyche can itself indicate that dreams are "sent" and that the images in them are used to convey indirectly something that cannot be shown or demonstrated directly.

We cannot know if such dreams finally indicate human survival over bodily death, even though it is a universal archetypal theme. As a research question, survival after death is an immensely complicated affair. J.B. Rhine points this out in an address to the Texas Society for Psychical Research, which happened to fall on Easter Sunday, 1977. He says:

> When I was a child I remember the concept of Easter as being a day of the promise of the literal resurrection. But by the time I went to high school, it was a symbolic resurrection. By the time I got to college, where I was a pre-ministerial student, the concept was something else; not resurrec-

tion but a promise of a spiritual existence of some kind that wasn't very clear. Further on in my college career, I had to throw the whole thing out. I didn't know what to accept. I couldn't see the basis for any of it in my studies in the sciences, to which I was drawn very strongly, especially psychology and biology. Still further on, by this time a graduate student, I heard about mediums and psychical research and the idea that life after death was something, an existence with which you could come to terms—you could do something about it.[34]

Dr. Rhine then went on to review the history and frustration of his attempts to research the question of survival after death. There seemed at first to be striking evidence from mediums that surviving disincarnate personalities could convey information to living persons, but the investigation became almost impossible to interpret. This was because evidence for extrasensory perception by the living became much more convincing. It appeared uncertain whether the medium was receiving messages from actual surviving personal agencies, or was unconsciously dramatizing spirit communication using information gained by the medium's own extrasensory perception (ESP) from living persons and existing sources. Because of these difficulties in interpretation, Rhine finally abandoned direct investigation of the survival question and focused his efforts instead on the laboratory investigation of *psi* (ESP) abilities in living subjects. In his Easter Sunday address, however, he again took up the survival question and in fact gave some suggestions as to how it might be approached experimentally.

I had the opportunity to discuss the question of survival after death with Marie-Louise von Franz in late summer of 1989. Even though she was ill, she was kind enough to have tea with me at her country retreat in the little Swiss farming community of Bollingen, the same village where Jung built his tower. There was no electricity and the tea kettle was boiling over an open fire on the hearth.

Since Dr. von Franz had delved more deeply than anyone I knew into the questions of dreams and the meaning of death, I asked for her personal views. Like a true empiricist, she said: "When the time comes for my own death, then I will know—or perhaps I won't be there at all and can't ask the question." I pressed the point by asking about the possibility of reincarnation. "If there is reincarnation," I wondered, "what kind of person would you like to come back as and where would you like to be born?" She paused a moment and then stated emphatically: "I want to come back as myself!"

I took this as a very fitting reply to an impossible question. "Being oneself" is, after all, the meaning of Jung's primary understanding of life as the unfolding process of individuation: realizing in actual life one's innate potentiality. I believe Dr. von Franz both knows and exemplifies that truth.

Chapter 4

The "Buddhism" of Dreams

A NOTE ON "I"

While the Self, the dream-maker, is the theoretical center of the psyche, we experience everything through the sense of "I." "I" is the tacit component of all that I see, I hear, I feel, I think, or I dream. Even in a dream with no representation of the self, there remains the viewpoint of "I" from which the action of the dream is experienced.

"I" is the word which indicates ego, the conscious self. But ego is itself mysterious. Jung once called the ego a relatively constant personification of the psyche. On another occasion he used the metaphor of a king. The king did not found his kingdom, and may be unaware of all that the kingdom contains, yet he is the only ruler available and cannot abdicate. When the ego-king abdicates, without bearing the stress, severe neurosis or even psychosis can occur.

It may sound like mere word games, but we must understand that "I" is not the same as "myself." This is even expressed in the common English expression, "I am not myself today," suggesting that "I," the present speaker and the central point of immediate consciousness, is not at the moment ("today") identical with its usual and expected presentation of itself. Enfolded in this simple everyday phrase is a basic mystery of the human psyche: how can a conscious "I" occur amid all the flux of existence?

The Buddhist answer is that there is, in fact, no enduring

self, while Christianity has traditionally held to the belief of an immortal soul that is eternal and unchanging as long as God wills it so. But what is the "soul" in psychological terms? How can I *have* a soul? And how can I lose it?

We learned in chapter 1 that Jung sometimes referred to the anima/animus as "soul images" because the loss of these psychic contents, through projection onto someone else, felt like the description in native societies of "loss of soul." We also discussed the fact that the anima/animus might be looked upon as the field that manifests the principle of relationship, relating the personal sphere, where the ego-self is "king," with all that is "outside"—both in the outer world or in the deeper layers of the psyche.

While "I," which refers to the immediate sense of the self, is based upon the Self, the "soul" refers to a sense of connection which is based upon the field of the anima/animus. Some Jungian writers use "soul" and "psyche" in a rather mysterious and mystifying fashion. By and large they seem to mean that people who need more "soul" are out of touch with their own unconscious, and with themselves generally. Such people often convey a sense of superficiality to those who try to interact closely with them.

Theoretically, all contents of the psyche are a part of the original Self, which unfolds to produce the archetypal fields and is the archetype of the ego/self. Therefore, all psychic parts, at a deep level, have connections that tend toward individuation. Because consciousness of the ego/self entails a degree of freedom, being human is not simply the mechanical unfolding of innate potentials. We make choices and thereby live our own lives with some intentionality.

Our psychological difficulties often arise from an over-identification with the images we have constructed of ourselves. When we identify "I" too closely with a self-image, we constrict the true range and complexity of the psyche. Dreams then come as compensation, reminding us of the "other," the side of ourselves which has been left out. For instance, one person who felt inadequate and constricted had a series of dreams that showed her in the company of Queen Elizabeth. The opposite is true as well. A man who wished to ignore his own lack of emotional grounding dreamed of a supersonic jet that was trying to take off with horses' hooves for wheels.

Both the construction of a strong self and the realization of the limits of the self are necessary for psychological health and maturity. "I" identifies with "myself," but then a newer and more complete "myself" arises, requiring "I" to dis-identify from the first image and identify with the second. Between image one and image two, "I" feels something like a trapeze artist, precariously suspended in air as he moves (hopefully) from one trapeze to another.

In the best outcome, "I" comes to learn that there is no final and fixed resting place for personal identity. And this is acceptable, because individuation is now experienced as a process in which "myself" is engaged, more so than the particular images with which "I" is identified at a given time. Anyone who has looked at old photographs of himself will have experienced what I am describing. The photograph is an authentic representation of what was the self, now seen from the viewpoint of, and in a sense, incorporated into, the present "real" self.

Jung describes this dis-identification of "I" (from an over-identification with any image) as the center of the psyche, moving from the ego toward the Self. In finding that midpoint, the spiration of ego and Self, there is no better instructor than our own dreams. In them we identify and dis-identify again and again with a moving and meaningful pattern of images presented to the self by the Self.

CHRISTIAN AND BUDDHIST STRUCTURES IN DREAMS

We have looked at various forms in which the image of "God" may appear in dreams, and have seen that the dream-making function of the psyche can use the god-image to express something of recurrent importance. The fact that dreams produce some god-images from cultures and religions other than the dreamer's suggests that the dream-making center, the Self, has access to appropriate images of god far beyond the conscious knowledge of the dreamer.

The notion of "God" or "gods" may well be the most common and central aspect of most religious viewpoints. But Buddhism, one of the major religions of the world, does not acknowledge "God" as its most comprehensive term. Rather, one of the more central Buddhist concepts, especially in Zen, is *Sunyata*, or "emptiness." There are many sects and divisions of Buddhism, of course, just as there are of Christianity. In some, such as in "Pure Land" Buddhism, the figure of the *bodhisattva* is more central and functions much like a savior "god." Even here, however, the gods are part of *maya*, the illusion of the universe. They live longer and are more powerful than men, but they too, nevertheless, are impermanent. Ultimately all things are characterized by "emptiness." This concept of *Sunyata* does not indicate meaninglessness. Nor should it, as Zen philosopher Nishitani points out, evoke an experience of "nihility," the fear of non-being.[35] The "field of emptiness," according to Nishitani, is actually the ground from which all manifestation arises and where every "thing" exists on its own home ground, together with all other things in existence. Things appear by a process of "dependent co-arising," meaning that all things condition all other things.[36]

Because Buddhism, along with Christianity, is a major world religion, I have been interested in how the concept of emptiness (*Sunyata*) might be found in dreams. I have encountered dreams of Buddha, of course, and of other figures, such as the *bodhisattva* Manjusri. Yet, how might "emptiness" be represented in a dream?

I would suggest that emptiness appears in the *structure* of the dream itself, not in any particular image, scene, or action within the dream. Unrepresented itself, "emptiness" appears as the freedom and unpredictability of the dream imagery, meaningfully arising in a surprising manner. An opening scene often introduces a problem in the dream. The dream-self takes an action, or even an attitude toward the events, and the scene changes to a second scene, and so on. In this way, scenes and the plot of the dream develop.

The dream is not thus simply an epiphenomenon of brain activity, nor does it appear to be totally formed before the dream begins. Rather, the dream creates a dialogue between the dream-self and the other contents of the dream. The actions (or lack of actions) on the part of the dream-self are responded to by the dream-maker, the Self, within the ongoing dream. This sometimes takes place over the course of several dreams in the same night, or even over a longer series of related dreams over many nights.

In comparing Christianity and Buddhism, we may note first that the central image of Christianity is the cross, representing the crucifixion of Christ. The cross also implies the complete archetypal pattern of death (crucifixion) and transformation (resurrection). It is also a symbol of being suspended between the opposites of heaven and earth, as well as between the opposites of right and left, and conscious and unconscious. The central Christian image is therefore one of suffering transformation—transformation achieved through bearing tension.

The central Buddhist image, in contrast, is that of Buddha sitting in reposeful meditation, withdrawing from the conflict of opposites. Traditionally, the historical Buddha tried many

Grunewald's "The Crucifixion" brutally depicts the agony of Christ on the cross.

The Buddha, seated in the lotus position, prepares to share his wisdom with suffering humanity.

The central Christian image of the crucifixion is an image of suffering transformation. By contrast, the central Buddhist image is one of meditation and detachment from worldly pain.

types of ascetic suffering and denial of the body before abandoning such practices as fruitless. He then attained enlightenment while seated in long meditation beneath a tree. This image suggests something quite opposite to the suffering transformation of the crucifixion. The Buddhist model is one of detachment from the illusions of the world, illusions that lead only to pain, according to the eastern tradition. Conversely, pain is represented as integral to the path of transformation in the image of the cross.

These two central religious images of west and east—suffering transformation on the cross and freedom from painful attachment through meditation—meet in one of the alchemical phrases that Jung was fond of repeating: the instruction to "dissolve and coagulate." A closely related alchemical operation was the *circulatio*, in which the *prima materia*, the basic "stuff" was sublimated or made vaporous inside a strangely shaped glass *vas*. After sublimation, it cooled and returned to its original solid or liquid state, only to have the process repeated in an endless circle.

Circulatio took place in a special alchemical vessel that was sealed entirely once the *prima materia* was inserted. The top of the vessel became a tube of increasingly narrow diameter bent back, like a bird tucking its head under its wing, and reconnected with the wider portion of the container near its base. The alchemists called this special vessel a "pelican" because of its shape. The pelican—the bird—is also one of the traditional symbols of Christ. It was believed that the pelican fed its young with blood drawn from its own body, just as Christ's blood was the image of salvation for humankind.

Here I am attempting to weave together several strands of symbolism—religious, alchemical and psychological—in order to draw a clearer analogy to the structure of dreams and thus to understand their religious meaning. Dreams of heroic struggle (i.e., dragon fights or great battles) contain images that corre-

Figura XXXVII.

Exaltatio V. Essentiæ

Alchemists called their most important vessel a "pelican," because of the vessel's shape. Above: In this medieval text, a pelican is depicted inside an alchemical vessel. The pelican was believed to feed its young with blood drawn from its own breast; for this reason it was held to be a symbol of Christ.

spond to the figure of Christ who, in eastern liturgies, "over-comes Death with death"; Christ meets the death-dragon in its lair and triumphs over it through the resurrection. Scenes of vivid confrontation in dreams take this same "coagulating" Christian form: coming into contact with the opposites and enduring the tension of the struggle between them.

Dreams of release have a Buddhist tone, and are suggestive of the alchemical *solutio:* dissolving, putting into solution, and dispersing in the unconscious. The dream-self may be in severe straits when suddenly the release comes: the scene changes, the action shifts, or the dream-self wakes up or becomes lucid in the dream (i.e., he realizes it is a dream but continues dreaming).*

The two alchemical symbols of "dissolving" and "coagulating," as I have suggested, are roughly similar to the central images of Buddhism and Christianity, respectively. Both symbols are combined strikingly in the only perfectly symmetrical dream I have ever encountered:

> I am watching a boy who is himself watching a smooth river that flows steadily from horizon to horizon. Now I am the boy watching the river. Suddenly, I—the boy—am *in* the river, which is turbulent and full of clumpy objects. At the very moment I think I will drown in the river, I again become the boy watching the river, which is once more calm and smooth. Just before the dream ends, I assume a detached point of view, and am again watching the boy who is watching the river.

In this unusual dream, the beginning and end have the flavor of Buddhist detachment, while the central scene of the boy in the turbulent river has the Christian tone of struggle.

---

* See "Lucid Dreaming and Active Imagination: Implications for Jungian Therapy," by James A. Hall and Andrew Brylowski in *Quadrant* (Aug./Sept. 1991).

To conclude this chapter of religious and psychological interweaving, I would like to draw a final parallel between the process of analysis and individuation and the concept of *kenosis* in Christian theology. Basically, *kenosis* is the notion that Christ incarnated by "emptying" himself of his divinity. By removing the divine—the archetypal—from his personality, he was able to be "conceived of the Holy Ghost" and be "born of the Virgin Mary." This idea of *kenosis* would imply that Christ did not *become* divine after his resurrection; he simply recalled or resumed the divinity from which he had temporarily separated himself by *kenosis*.[37]

Since the archetypes may appear as gods, and the Self may assume the symbolic imagery of God, one might suggest that, like *kenosis* in theology, the ego/self arises through the Self, the original unity, emptying itself of its archetypal potentials while at the same time identifying with the experiences which form complexes. The ego/self that we indicate in speech as "I" always occurs in identification with some structure of complexes, while the opposite of those identity complexes tends to be in the shadow and appears as though it is outside the person and belongs to someone else. Similarly, complexes that are so different as not to belong to the ego, persona, or shadow, are projected onto the anima/animus, opposite in sex from the ego/self.

We have noted that in everyday life we make statements such as "I am not myself today." Being "myself" means that I am comfortably identified, for now, with the complexes that I feel are part of my basic nature. In that usual state we do not realize that "I," the center of our consciousness based on the Self, could also be identified with a different selection of complexes. But we experience this separation of "I" and our identity when something happens to disturb our usual and comfortable sense of who we are. Something may change outside us, in other persons or in the environment, or something may change within us. Such changes from within may reflect the Self's activity, which moves the ego/self toward an enlargement of its own personal sphere. By holding on to certain complexes, we form our identity. By letting go of those firm identifications we allow a newer identity to form. The innate thrust of the human psyche seems to be in the direction of that new identity which is more comprehensive, larger, and closer to "the true self." There is always, however, the danger of regression and backward movement.

Both holding on and letting go are necessary for life, like the systole and diastole of the heartbeat, or the inspiration and expiration of breathing. The reality is the *process*, for which both extremes are needed. When the waking-self, perhaps through the instruction of its dreams, learns that it is itself carried by the individuation process, there is a simultaneous deepening of the self and an opening of the world.

cf Chopra re the intelligence (The Self ?) beyond everything

Chapter 5

Self: The Dream-Maker

In approaching the questions raised by the image of God in dreams, I have used terms such as "gods" and "god-image" in the usual manner of Jungian literature: that is, to refer to the variety of images of God in various mythologies and religious systems. From a purely psychological point of view, gods and god-images are personified archetypes. But archetypes, the organizing fields of our experiences, themselves arise from the central archetype, which is the Self. I will now consider this central concept of the Self more closely, and explore some of the evidence for it.

Harold Coward, the scholar of eastern religions, has shown how Jung's concept of Self developed over the long course of his life.[38] Early in life, Jung was influenced by the Hindu concept of ātman, which refers to both the small personal self and the larger transpersonal Self. Later, Jung further developed his notion of the Self in reference to the western alchemical image of the philosopher's stone—the *lapis*. This image represented, Jung believed, a medieval psychological compensation, projected onto matter, for the official image of Christ. Alchemy was also the historical precursor of chemistry and other sciences; physicists can now literally change lead into gold, but not at a profitable rate of energy expenditure. What Jung found uniquely was the precursor of depth psychology in the visions of the alchemists.

After a serious illness in 1944, Jung devoted the rest of his life to exploring the archetypal foundations of the human psyche. One of his major works of this final period is *Aion*, which he subtitled, "Researches into the Phenomenology of the Self."[39] In his concluding discussion of the Self in *Aion*, Jung makes several interesting points.

Above all, the Self is a *process*, not a static end point. It appears to be a self-regenerating process that moves the conscious self along the path of individuation toward the realization of its own innate potentialities. The final goal, if there is one, is mysterious, although it can be spoken of in metaphors such as the union of body, mind, and spirit; the achievement of the alchemical lapis; or, as in Chinese Taoist alchemy, the "golden flower." In *Aion*, Jung indicates through diagrams that the Self involves the body as well as the psyche. A major part of the process is the discrimination of good and evil ("Christos" and "Diabolos" in Jung's model), although that tension between the two is diminished when the Self is seen, in its "ouroboric" form, as a process rather than a fixed thing.

The tensions of male and female also are innate in the Self, manifesting as the anima/animus in the human personality. One may always achieve a higher state, and avoid regression to a lower state. Yet in some sense the highest and the lowest are virtually the same, just as in alchemy, the highest value is innate in the alchemical *rotundum*, the original but confused unity of all things. The most unusual point of all is that the Self can be read as both personal and transpersonal, an attribute that may open the Self to empirical approaches.

Seen from a theoretical viewpoint, Jung's theory of the Self is one among many self theories.[40] Like all theories, it explains a certain limited range of phenomena. Yet it is my contention that Jung's theory of the Self is the most comprehensive.[41] Three lines of evidence have convinced me that Jung's view of the Self is essentially correct. These are (1) the meaningfulness that unfolds when one examines at close range lives that appear, from the outside, commonplace; (2) the relation of dreams to conscious life, as seen from a classical Jungian point of view; and (3) the evidence for synchronicity; parapsychological events such as telepathy, clairvoyance, precognition (particularly in dreams); and psychokinesis (the influence of mind on matter).

MEANINGFULNESS

(¹)

One of the cardinal rules in writing fiction is that the plot must not seem to turn on "acts of God," *deus ex machina*. When I studied playwriting at the University of Texas, my professor, E.P. Conkle, taught that everything in a script must be motivated. The audience needs to understand why a particular character acts the way he or she does, and it has to make sense in terms of the audience's perception of that character. The only exception Professor Conkle allowed was this: any type of person may be married to any other type of person without clear motivation because audiences have observed this in their everyday lives!

The psychotherapist cannot leave even marriages to chance, for a basic part of understanding a person's life in depth is to gain some sense of why that person has had the kinds of marriages, or relationships, that have actually occurred. Often this leads to an understanding of the development of the anima/ animus in the person. Even so, in looking at lives with close observation, as in analysis, events often seem to violate the rule against *deus ex machina*. It is often as if a person's life were plotted by a poor novelist, full of unexpected events that are meaningful—events that, if they occurred in fiction, would be attributed to the manipulation of events by the author.

Psychotherapists often remark, for example, that the patients that come to them are somehow just the right ones to make them aware of their *own* problems. Or, it is sometimes noted that two patients with apparently different problems will arrive at the same psychotherapy group to discover that they have unexpected convergence in their lives, so that one's life experience seems to enlighten the other's.

How does this occur? Is it simply happenstance? My view is that the Self, which controls projections as much as it controls our dreams, uses the unconscious process of projection to call the attention of the conscious mind to events and persons that are needed for the next stages of personality development. This can even work in the choice of one psychotherapist over another, and is particularly evident in the projection of the positive anima/animus. The person whose unconscious is making the projection causes the conscious self to become aware of certain persons in the environment, those who can "carry" the specific projections that are needed for the next stage of anima/animus development.

When this projection process is carried too far, however, as in psychosis, it disrupts the working relation of the ego and the Self. It is then that one sees the underlying mechanisms of archetypal projection in their more pure form. Even there, it is often possible to follow the renewal process that the Self is attempting in images that imply a reconstitution of a stable ego consciousness.[42] These are often images that have been associated with kingship, since the king is the carrier of the archetypal projection of the Self in the kingdom he rules. We are seldom aware of such projections except when there is a sudden interruption of the process, when the archetypal foundation shows through in dreams and in irrational behavior. I observed this phenomena myself when President Kennedy was assassinated. One of my patients behaved as if his castrating oedipal father were suddenly removed; another relived the loss of her brother during World War II.

CONSCIOUSNESS AND THE DREAM-MAKER

What is seen over an extended period of time in the meaningful movements of lives can be seen in cross-section, as it were, in dreams. Earlier we looked at images of gods or divine figures in dreams. The ordinary experience of a series of dreams in Jungian analysis, however, is quite different. Instead of looking for particular motifs, one finds in a series of dreams an ongoing counterpoint to the attitudes and movements of conscious life. Recurring motifs can be identified over months and years. They often represent the gradual incorporation of certain contents into consciousness.

There may be a dream in which a fish appears, for example, but when it is brought out of the water it becomes a companion, sits by the campfire, and converses with the dream self. Later, in the same person's dreams, a dog appears and speaks to him. Still later, an infant appears, sometimes with the ability to speak. This progression, intuitively chosen from a long series of dreams of the same person, shows how a content arises from the unconscious (the fish), then achieves a status closer to consciousness (the dog, companion to mankind), and finally takes on human form (the infant).

It is impossible to convey the complexity of dream life in even a single individual. Yet, by observing the dreams of many persons within the ongoing context of their lives, one can see that the dream-maker, the Self, has an unusual relationship to the waking-self. First, the Self is very familiar with the experiences of the self and is able to tie together, to one's conscious surprise, present events with similar events from the past. Furthermore, dreams are capable of making profound statements that startle consciousness, such as the man who dreamt of a voice saying, "You are not leading your true life!" Dreams lead the waking-self onward, correct it, joke about its foibles, but never abandon it or show indifference to it. This is true even when the concerns of the dream-maker are not those of the waking-self, as can be seen in dreams of persons approaching physical death, as we have previously discussed.

Overall, the dream-maker is like a very intimate, yet objective and wise friend. It is like someone who will tell the waking-self what is true from the perspective of the Self, but will always do this in the spirit of wisdom and helpfulness. I picture the relation of the Self to the waking-self very much like the relationship of the hexagrams in the *I Ching*, the ancient Chinese book of oracles and philosophy to which Jung wrote an introduction.[43] The hexagrams of the *I Ching* always suggest what the sage, the "superior man," would do in a particular situation. Sometimes it helps one to make a major change, "to cross the great water," while at other times it suggests that "nothing furthers." There is never criticism or moralizing, but always a gentle reminder of what action would be appropriate from the most human viewpoint which one might take, that of the sage.

Dreams are similar in tone, always trying to find a workable way for the waking-self to progress along the path of individuation. Only when the waking-self is excessively resistant to unconscious guidance, and then for a long while, do dreams seem to adopt an attitude inimical to the self. In one striking initial dream, the dream-self was viciously attacked. But this led the ego to fight back with a weapon, and thereby reawakened much content thought to be "dead." Von Franz has discussed the only example known to me personally in which the dream-maker seems to have given up on the dreamer. The dream she cites is of an "international criminal" who had killed a number of people in cold blood. His dream showed him falling out of a swing into absolute nothingness.

As difficult as it is to interpret dreams rationally (dream interpretation is still an art), the study of dreams provides one of the most convincing avenues of evidence for the Self—the dream-maker. The center of the human psyche is a wise, caring, but objective friend, focused not upon what one wants, but upon what one truly needs in order to proceed along the path of individuation. And the Self is the core of the self that proceeds.

SYNCHRONICITY

In the last period of his life, Jung also wrote about "synchronicity."[44] In his practice, he had long observed many striking and apparently coincidental events which seemed, nevertheless, to have a more meaningful connection than one of mere chance. In one instance, Jung was discussing with a resistant patient her dream of a scarab, when he noticed a scarab-like beetle trying to come into the room through the window glass. Both Jung and the patient were startled. The event resulted in the patient taking a deeper and more earnest interest in her analytical process.[45]

Jung felt that the work of J.B. Rhine, the founder of parapsychology as a science, offered experimental proof for the synchronistic phenomena he had observed clinically, just as Jung's work with the word-association experiment seemed to offer some scientific support for Freud's early psychoanalytic work. In his essay on synchronicity, Jung cites extensively the work of Rhine at the Parapsychology Laboratory at Duke University. Having reviewed some of the unpublished correspondence between Jung and Rhine in the Rhine archives at Duke, I believe that it was at the urging of Rhine that Jung finally published his thoughts about synchronicity.

Jung's strong interest in Rhine's laboratory study of parapsychology indicates the importance which Jung attached to synchronicity. He describes it as an "acausal connecting principle" which must be considered along with our usual conscious view of causation. In his study on synchronicity, Jung defined the archetype as "psychoid." Previously, he had presented the archetype as if it were an ordering principle only in the psyche, with an "infrared" pole of instinctual behavior and an "ultraviolet" pole of imagery. The new term "psychoid" meant that one simply cannot tell, in the final analysis, whether an archetype is an ordering principle of the psyche, of matter, or of both. The laboratory results of Rhine's work on ESP provided the empirical evidence used to substantiate this expanded view of archetypal patterning. Jung's new thesis made sense of the long-standing observation that parapsychological events seem to take place when "an archetype is constellated," at times such as severe distress and death.

Although there is not enough evidence in parapsychology to compel someone to believe in *psi* phenomena when he or she wishes deeply to doubt them, there is, in my judgment, sufficient evidence to give strong support to someone who does accept their existence. The laboratory results of experiments in parapsychology, together with the extensive anecdotal evidence from all cultures, create a compelling case.

The Self, the source of archetypes, extends its influence from the world of consciousness to the world of matter, as can be seen in Jung's *Aion* diagrams. When we add that the Self represents itself in dreams through images of god, it becomes increasingly apparent that we are, at our own core, connected to the universe we inhabit in ways more profound than we can imagine. At the center of the human psyche is a wise, caring, but completely objective Self. The same Self may be at the core not only of our bodies, but of the world as well.

Chapter 6

The Unconscious Christian:
A Reprise

We have now looked at many images of God in dreams and have seen the great variety of forms in which they appear. Like the epiphanies of a deity described in a religious text, the meaning of a dream-image of God may be difficult to discern. Although some god-images in dreams behave as they do in the conscious life of the dreamer, many do not. Images with definite places in known mythologies appear in dreams of persons who have no causal way of knowing that mythological context; and yet the personal meaning of the god-image in the individual's dream is also appropriate to its mythological meaning. We have spoken of this mysterious appearance of mythological images in terms of Jung's theory of archetypes; but a shaman in a tribal society might consider them actual entities in the spirit world. Who is to say with certainty which is correct?

Some of these mythological god-images are strangely efficacious and therapeutic: recall the powerful curative effect on the patient who dreamed of removing from a canal a hippopotamus-like monster with a crocodile's pointed head! We have also seen that the structure of a dream itself suggests an organizing center in the psyche. This center, which Jung called the Self, is the maker of all dreams. When it is symbolized, it often appears as an image of God. We have also seen that the very form of a dream may have certain Buddhist resonances. The meaningful "co-arising" of images in a dream reminds one of the activity of

Sunyata, or "emptiness," in Buddhism. Finally, throughout I have suggested the possibility that the psyche has an innate religious function which affects even persons who hold no conscious religious belief or interest. The effects of suppressing such a function can be pathological, as religious expression may thus follow less direct routes to consciousness.

Our title, "The Unconscious Christian," is restated in this final chapter. This is because persons in our culture are often unconscious of their own religious quests. These quests often appear in our dreams and unconscious productions, such as fantasy and art. It is as though the religious question pursues its course in the underworld reality of dreams, having been consciously abandoned by so many persons in the present age. I do not doubt that there are also "unconscious Buddhists" and other such persons from non-Christian religions as well. The behavior of god-images in dreams suggests that the innate religious function in the psyche is concerned less with the particular form of a religion and its images than with the healing potential and appropriateness of those images, regardless of their tradition of origin.

I would like to conclude with a final clinical example, this time involving hypnosis rather than dreaming. A man had been in individual and group Jungian analysis for several years. Divorced for some time, he had gradually developed a sense of competence in work and in close personal relationships with women. He regularly attended a Protestant church and for a time considered going to seminary to become a minister. His dreams ranged widely—in one he was protected from "the devil" by "the devil's daughter."

Although he knew of my interest in hypnosis, hypnotherapy had not been a part of his treatment.[46] One day he went to an all-day seminar on hypnosis. Early in the seminar he said to a female friend, a former lover, that he wondered what it would be like to be a hypnotic subject. Encouraged by her, he volunteered and was chosen for a demonstration of hypnotic induction.

The technique was very permissive. He was asked to let his hands act autonomously of his conscious will, allowing them to indicate if he had a problem to work on at that time, and the willingness of his unconscious mind to do such work. His hands moved spontaneously and slowly. From an almost clasped position, they moved slowly outward. In some ten minutes, as they approached the position of his shoulders, he began to cry. Although he was experiencing spontaneous imagery, he did not wish to share it with the sixty persons in the seminar, most of whom were unknown to him. The demonstration ended by his confirming that he had come into contact with an important problem within himself, but did not wish to share it with the seminar participants.

In his next hour of individual analysis, he discussed what had happened during the hypnosis demonstration. As his hands moved outward, he began to feel as if he were being crucified. This image brought up not only religious feelings, but a sense of such personal pain and passion that he did not wish to reveal it in the impersonal setting of the seminar. In the individual analytic hour, he asked if hypnotherapy might be used to finish the process that began with the hypnosis demonstration. A light trance was induced and for twenty minutes he tried to get back into the feeling of the trance motif of crucifixion. It was not possible, however, to re-create and work with this material, and it was suggested that he continue his work alone at home if he wished.

At his next appointment, he described what had happened when he worked with this spontaneous imagery alone at home. He had gone back into the imaginal situation, much as in hypnosis, and for more than two hours was engaged in a deep struggle within himself. As his hands slowly began to spread outward into the form of a cross, he felt fear, awe, and uncertainty. After perhaps an hour, they reached their most extended position and he waited apprehensively for what might happen next.

Just as slowly as his hands had reached the cruciform position, they began to come back toward his face. This constellated the most profound anxiety of the entire experience. It suddenly occurred to him that his hands, which seemed to function autonomously, might try to strangle him. A sudden and awful thought occurred to him: could that be God's will? What was he to do? Although he knew he could break the self-induced trance state, he did not will to do so. In the midst of his uncertainty, he decided to abandon himself to whatever was going to happen.

His hands came closer to his throat. With as much sincerity as he had ever felt in the presence of a crucial decision, he decided to accept whatever happened as the will of God. In this moment, he abandoned himself. He trusted something within himself that he neither understood nor willed. Just as he was about to feel his own hands upon his throat, they began again to move outward in the form of a cross. Relief! But then came the sense that perhaps the whole process would repeat again. How many times would it recur?

This entire meditative experience, as he reported it, comprised more than two hours. It had a profound impact upon him. He felt a powerful tension between the will of his conscious self and something else, deep within him. The religious imagery of the crucifixion had been personalized. Moreover, it was relativized, seen as part of a recurrent cycle of stress and release. Far from changing his traditional Christian beliefs, it provided a new and challenging religious space in which he could work out the religious impulse within him in a quite personal way. Perhaps the experience also enhanced his understanding of others who might be on their own quest for personal religious meaning amid the traditional images of western culture.

He readily gave permission to quote his experience for the purposes of this book. He is another "unconscious Christian," as perhaps many of us are. In addition to revelation, tradition, and church community, he discovered that, in his own inner experience, the image of God works in meaningful but mysterious ways.

May we each find our own path, outward if possible, inward if necessary. And in all cases may our movement along this path give us a sense of the encompassing yet personal mystery that remains even nearer to us than our dreams.

Appendix: Is There an Innate Religious Function in the Psyche?

Gradually I have become convinced, on the basis of my clinical experience as a Jungian analyst, that Jung was right in believing that there is a natural religious function in the psyche. Religion, or at least spirituality, is more than the illusory projections of the irrational and unpsychological masses, as Freud portrays religion in his famous book, *The Future of an Illusion*. My conviction rests in part upon the healing activity of religious images in dreams, such as those discussed in this volume. However, even if there were no dreams to study, the existence of an innate religious function in the psyche is still suggested strongly in the movement of neurotic persons out of their neuroses. The analytic process gives one an intimate view of a person's life over an extended period. One comes to see clearly that a person with neurosis is trapped by self-rejection. Like the comedian Groucho Marx, he or she is saying essentially: "I wouldn't belong to any club that would accept me as a member." No one other than himself can free the neurotic person from this trap: neither therapist, parent, nor loving partner.

In addition to my own observation of dreams, this conviction is based upon the work of both Jung, in depth psychology, and of Michael Polanyi, in epistemology and the philosophy of science. Jung was concerned with the relation of consciousness to the unconscious, particularly the relation of the personal conscious psyche to the objective psyche (the collective unconscious). Polanyi was concerned with the actual nature of scientific discovery, which he found to have an irreducible component of personal commitment and risk.

Polanyi focused on the structure of scientific understanding and insight, which he described as the focal/tacit structure of all knowing. For Polanyi all knowledge was inevitably personal knowledge, even if it was asserted as universally valid.

Jung understood the most basic process of human life as individuation, by which he meant the tendency of the human psyche to unfold its innate possibilities. As I mentioned in an earlier chapter, Jung is quoted often as saying that he never saw a patient in the second half of life who did not have a religious problem. By "religious problem" Jung meant a problem of meaning in life. When the ordinary tasks of maturation of the personality are accomplished, there still remain questions of transpersonal value and the final meaning or meaninglessness of life. The ego-development of the first half of life moves toward a zenith of establishing oneself in the world; the movement of the second half of life requires an attitude toward finitude and death. Questions of the second half of life, therefore, move inevitably toward religious formulations.

It is important to realize that the questions which guide the first and second halves of life are not the same. Questions of the first half admit some empirical answers, for they are posed within a certain culture according to a given role in that culture; and they draw on a finite but real amount of personal energy and effort. Real possibilities can be pursued and, to some degree, actualized.

Once past the zenith of life, however, the type of questions, and the style of answer, must change. While worldly success (and failure, its inevitable accompaniment), guide the first half of life, the goal or end point of the whole of life is inevitably death. This fact relativizes all systems of success and failure and raises questions of ultimate meaning. Described in different terms, goals of the first half of life exist within a frame of reference that is potentially knowable and alterable; questions of the second half of life concern the meaning and value of life itself, and thus are not subject to an empirical answer.

Polanyi's guiding insight was the personal nature of all knowing; hence he titled his major work *Personal Knowledge*.[47] All knowledge must be held by a mind, and is therefore personal. All knowledge that is meant to be objective must also be held by one or more minds and is unavoidably personal, although it may be held with universal intent, intent that it shall also be found true by any other person who pursues truth objectively. The pursuit of truth, however, is itself a personal quest, a quest involving personal commitment and passion. The image of scientific enquiry as a dispassionate search for objective knowledge is dispelled by Polanyi's analysis.

In Polanyi's epistemology, all knowing has a form/to structure, relying upon tacit areas of knowledge in a peripheral manner, in order to know in a focal manner other areas of knowledge. To know a comprehensive entity, one dwells upon certain particulars of the entity so as to attend to the comprehensive entity to which those particulars are subsidiary clues. The recognition of someone's face, for example, often involves a skilled performance in perception which cannot be specified by exact rules. The same is true of all skilled performances.

The nature of scientific discovery, in Polanyi's view, is actually a process of selection guided by an intuition of a comprehensive entity which is not yet known. The "facts" function as clues, or particulars, of the entity that is becoming known.

In speaking of focal and tacit knowing, Polanyi does not equate them with the conscious or the unconscious. His epistemology does not oppose this distinction, nor is it exhausted by it.

Because all belief relies upon some unspecifiable tacit knowledge, and moves toward more comprehensive visions that also contain a tacit compartment of knowing, there is no final resting place for religious or scientific belief. It is, therefore, meaningless to attempt to eradicate the "truth" of religion by reference to a more exact "truth" of science. "The acceptance of the Christian faith," writes Polanyi, "does not express the assertion of observable facts and consequently you cannot prove or disprove Christianity by experiments or factual records."[48]

In a sense, Polanyi sees Christian faith embodying the essentially unfulfillable quest for comprehension, exalting God and simultaneously affirming the inability of the worshipper to know God.[49] In this vision God *might* stand for the movement toward comprehension itself, rather than the arrival of any particular comprehension. "God" could be said to be the vector toward more comprehensive knowing, a vector pointing from the current belief in a present "reality" toward an increasingly more comprehensive reality whose tacit components are more encompassing. Religious worship would seem to be an enactment of this structure of knowing itself, rather than the focal knowledge of any specifiable content.

Religious faith can be attacked in two ways, according to Polanyi.[50] One may question its internal consistency, in the same manner as one may question the relevance of a work of art; or one may question the particulars in which the religious faith is expressed: the "reality" of resurrection, for example. Destruction of the credibility of particulars which a faith embodies does not logically challenge the faith, but it does make indwelling in the *particular* religious vision more problematic.

I wish to present briefly the central ways in which the works of Jung and Polanyi, as sketched above, point jointly toward an innate religious function in mankind. Jung and Polanyi differ in their realms of interest: Jung is interested in a depth psychological understanding of the person; and Polanyi in the vast cultural sweep of science. Since the origins of their interests differ so greatly, the convergence of their thought upon the notion of a natural religious activity in the human mind is striking in itself. There are, however, other areas where the work of Jung and Polanyi more naturally converge. Both considered themselves to be working within the field of scientific inquiry, and both presented a view of reality in which religion is a natural, perhaps unavoidable, activity of mankind.

Polanyi saw science as a cooperative effort between many persons, where no one could possibly be competent to judge the validity of all others' work.[51] A society of scientists, therefore, arises: a network of individuals who rely upon colleagues who personally vouch for each other. This extends into a vast system of mutual trust and respect through adherence to commonly affirmed beliefs. The creativity of science, however, remains within the realm of individual vision and initiative. It is impossible to scientifically prescribe experiments that will yield novel scientific results. There is first a vision of increasing unity and order in the mind of a particular scientist. The vision may then be translated into experimental activities whose results may support the original vision. Confirmatory experiments can reveal evidence that extends the original vision into unforeseen ranges of understanding. Science reserves its highest honors for those individuals who give birth to new and more comprehensive understandings that relativize, but do not necessarily destroy, the models of understanding which they replace.

Jung places a similar emphasis upon the unique and creative activity of the individual. Society consists of individuals held together by archetypal images, unconsciously shared. New images can be integrated into the society only through the activity of individual minds. For Jung, individual change is thus the indispensable factor in social change. Only if a sufficient number of persons in a culture individuate can there be effective resistance to the continual currents of archetypal change that can disorganize social structure. The spread of National Socialism in Hitler's Germany illustrates the mechanism of shadow projection upon another country or racial group.

For Jung, as for Polanyi, there is no carrier of consciousness and no locus of creative emergence outside the individual human being. Objective knowledge for Polanyi can only be personal knowledge held with universal intent. While speaking of the vast potential and energy of archetypal forms, Jung continually emphasizes the crucial importance of the individual ego as the only container or effective agent of consciousness.

Polanyi and Jung converge also in their visions of the universe, and the human personality within it, as exhibiting a hierarchical structure. The activity of the higher levels depends upon, but is not determined by, the orderly working of lower levels. Lower levels support but do not determine the emergence of higher levels. Polanyi describes this hierarchical structure most convincingly in his analysis of machines.[52]

A new machine embodies a unique and creative arrangement of mechanical principals, imposed upon the materials from which the machine is constructed. Yet the parts of the machine are also governed by the laws of physics and chemistry; laws which deal with a different level of reality and are indifferent to the principles of mechanics upon which the machine is based.

The principles of physics and chemistry determine the physical and chemical properties of the materials of which the machine is constructed, but leave open the possibility of those materials supporting the embodiment of any number of different machines. Thus, the lower order principles of physics and chemistry do not determine the emergence of a machine. They allow such emergence by their indifference to the form in which the physical properties are embedded by the creative act of making a machine. Yet, because machines rely upon the orderly functioning of the physical and chemical properties of their constituents, changes at the lower physical and chemical level can cause the breakdown of machines. The lower orders of a comprehensive entity, therefore, can cause the entity's breakdown; however, the lower orders are not able in themselves to produce the emergence of a new comprehensive entity. Such emergence is always a creative act.

Jung was apparently unaware of Polanyi's writings, but his early work with the word-association experiment followed principles nearly parallel to Polanyi's analysis of the breakdown of a machine.[53] Jung focused upon missed or delayed responses in the word-association task, postulating that these interferences in the normal working of the conscious mind were due to excessive activity of aroused psychological complexes—associations of images held together by a common emotional tone. At the same time, the conscious mind is dependent upon complexes for its own structure. The ego itself is, according to Jung, one complex among many, but it is a unique complex which has the quality of consciousness.[54] Complexes other than the ego-self may behave as "part-personalities" with some degree of consciousness of their own.[55] The emergence of new ego-states, therefore, is a continually creative activity, involving moral risk and the possibility of error. This activity of the ego relies upon the orderly working of other complexes, which are in fact constituents of the waking-ego's image of itself and the world. Excessive, uncontrolled, or disorderly functioning of complexes, however, may disrupt the functioning of the waking personality, although such complexes cannot determine the personality's unique and unpredictable movement in the processes of individuation.

When the waking-ego, the self (lowercase "s"), is functioning properly, it can enter into a healthy relationship with the Self (capital "S")—the central archetype. The Self is the coordinating center of the psyche as a whole, whereas the ego (self) is seen as only the center of consciousness.[56] When symbols of the Self are perceived by the ego, they often appear with the same symbolism that is traditionally associated with a deity, as we have seen previously. The Self is to the ego as a comprehensive center is to a smaller center of consciousness contained within it: that is, as a complex in the personal sphere of the psyche is related to the ego-complex. This model of the ego (self) and Self is sufficient to illuminate many of the psychopathological observations of psychiatry, particularly the phenomenology of paranoic schizophrenia, where the waking-ego may assume the delusional identity of a divine figure (such as Christ) or of a culture hero (such as Napoleon). If Jung's model was not permeable to the world outside the psyche, it might simply function as a descriptive psychological system for normal and pathological functioning.

Jung was greatly concerned, as we saw earlier in this volume, with the question of synchronicity—a question which comprises much of the parapsychological studies done by J.B. Rhine and others. Synchronistic events—the occurrence in time of inner psychic events and outer events with the same meaning but no causal connection—point to an underlying unity of the mind and the world, a connection that Jung expressed with the term *unus mundus*, one world. While synchronicity describes sporadic and striking events, it points to the profound possibility of an underlying unity of mind and matter. It may be that such an underlying unity presents itself in novel developments in mathematics, for example, where a purely intuitive development in mathematical theory (which has no necessary connection to any observational data) is found by scientists to be useful in describing observable physical properties of the world.

Polanyi asserts that the universe is meaningful and that serious quests for more comprehensive understanding of this underlying order may produce new and convincing visions that compel assent.[57] The process of Jungian analysis involves the progressive intuition of comprehensive orders of meaning that unite previously dissociated parts of the psyche, such as the ego, the persona, and the shadow. Images of the Self may appear in dreams or imaginative productions, foreshadowing the emergence of an enlarged and more coherent personhood.

No perfect and final resting place is anticipated in either Polanyi or Jung. Each succeeding integration of previously disparate elements is merely the groundwork, the *prima materia*, for a successive and more comprehensive integration, which may itself be surpassed. The fantasy of a completed science, of a "Laplacian mind" that can contemplate the entire universe without error, is for Polanyi an impossibility.[58] For Jung, the individuation process never leads one to a complete and fully individuated state. The process of individuation is pictured as circumambulations of a mysterious center that can be intuitively known but not focally grasped. For Polanyi, the rituals of Christian worship permit the believing Christian to dwell in the mystery of finitude and transcendence, between which the tension is never resolved. For Jung, the relation of the ego to the more encompassing Self is a mystery that preserves the tension of the personal and the archetypal, always dynamic and emergent, never to be resolved in life.

In summary, there are three primary ways in which Jung's vision of individuation converges with Polanyi's vision of the scientific quest as personal knowledge:

1. There is a unity of world and mind, evidenced by developments in mathematics, by the occurrence of synchronicity, and by the continual possibility of the emergence of more comprehensive order.

2. The structure of the universe permits, if it does not require, a religious perspective on realities beyond our powers of focal and conscious knowing, however greatly expanded.

3. Human life is never removed from the ubiquitous possibility of the emergence of new and potentially more comprehensive integrations, whether in the personal world (Jung's

concern) or in the transpersonal enterprise of scientific inquiry, (as seen in Polanyi's work).

A final question: to what extent are these possibilities suggested by Jung and Polanyi subject to empirical investigation? Jung described the individuation process in terms of mythological systems as well as in terms of extended clinical case material. The individuation process can also be observed, as if in microscopic section, in dream material from ongoing analytic cases. Synchronicity, which Jung saw as revealing an underlying connection of the physical and the psychical, is studied in the field of parapsychology, whose scientific status seems increasingly assured. Polanyi's epistemology aspires to describe the underlying processes of all modern scientific thought.

If we exist in a universe in which religious values are inherent, this fact should be demonstrable, at least to the extent that one can illustrate the continuous unfolding of entities more comprehensive than the present self. Religious feeling is the intuitive perception of a vector of meaning moving toward transcendence of present tacit boundaries of understanding and meaning. The works of both Jung and Polanyi converge upon this problem from discretely different fields of study. Both Jung and Polanyi suggest that there is a natural religious function in the psyche, and therefore in the universe, as we are permitted to know and experience it.

Notes

1. In this case, as in all the case material presented in this book, I have used pseudonyms for all persons involved.
2. The Archetypal Self is at once the most central and the least empirical of Jung's concepts. It has been emphasized most strongly by the Zurich or "classical" school of Jungian psychology. A different emphasis is found among the British Jungians, the majority of whom have focused on questions of the Self within the developmental theories of childhood. A third branch of Jungian thought, often called "archetypal psychology," has taken a more phenomenological and deconstructionist approach, with less relevance to clinical practice. By and large the archetypalist Jungians have ignored the concepts of the *Self* and the *ego-Self axis*, as they are understood in the classical tradition, to which I belong. It is now becoming clear that archetypalist Jungians have a much more antinomian approach to the psyche than did Jung, who considered himself a physician and an empiricist.
3. Murray Stein, *Jung's Treatment of Christianity* (Wilmette Il: Chiron Publications, 1985).
4. *The Collected Works of C. G. Jung* (hereafter cited as *CW*), Bollingen Series XX, 20 vols., trans. R.F.C. Hull, eds. H. Read, M. Fordham, G. Adler, Wm. McGuire (Princeton: Princeton University Press, 1953–1979).
5. C. G. Jung, *Memories, Dreams, Reflections* (New York: Pantheon, 1961).
6. Ibid., 289–298.
7. Jung, *Answer to Job, CW* 11.
8. Jung, *Aion: Researches into the Phenomenology of the Self, CW*, vol. 9ii.

9. Jung, *Mysterium Coniunctionis: An Inquiry into the Separation and Synthesis of Psychic Opposites in Alchemy*, *CW* 14.
10. Jung, *Memories, Dreams, Reflections*.
11. C. G. Jung and M-L von Franz, eds., *Man and his Symbols* (New York: Doubleday, 1964).
12. Jung, "Studies in Word Association (1904-7, 1910)," *CW* 2.
13. The concept of de-integration is a contribution of Michael Fordham, a British Jungian who made a special study of infant development. Fordham's concept, I believe, follows Jung's own position closely. See Fordham, *The Objective Psyche* (London: Routledge & Kegan Paul, 1958), 62, 66.
14. See my thesis at the Jung Institute in Zurich, and Chapter 7 of Hall, *Clinical Uses of Dreams: Jungian Interpretations and Enactments* (New York: Grune & Stratton, 1977).
15. See Hall, *Clinical Uses of Dreams*, 174-177.
16. From the French film *Orpheus*, released in 1949, written and directed by Jean Cocteau. The words are spoken by the princess, an image of death.
17. See C. A. Meier, *Ancient Incubation and Modern Psychotherapy*, trans. M. Curtis (Evanston: Northwestern University Press, 1967).
18. Genesis 41:1-32.
19. See R. DeBecker, *The Understanding of Dreams, or the Machinations of the Night*, trans. M. Heron (London: Allen & Unwin, 1968), 19-61.
20. Other schools have seen the manifest dream in a different light. The existential-phenomenalistic approach views the dream as indicating areas of personality constriction that narrow the range of conscious response, not only in the dream but in waking life as well. In a similar manner, humanistic and transpersonal writers generally view the dream as showing ranges of integration greater than that currently achieved in consciousness.
21. See Hall, *Clinical Uses of Dreams*, 269.
22. E. C. Keeler, *Secrets of the Cuña Earthmother: A Comparative Study of Ancient Religions* (New York: Exposition Press, 1960).
23. I have since seen the large tapir motif in the dreams of at least one of my analysands. Although it was not as striking as the parallel I

experienced in my own dream, in his dream, too, the tapir seemed to be associated with a positive mother complex and its attendant difficulties. I have collected other striking parallels between similar archetypal images in the dreams of different persons.

24. This kind of dream image can be handled quite well in analysis without knowing its archetypal meaning, yet it poses important theoretical problems. My own Sullivanian analyst made perfectly good use of the tapir dream within this frame of reference. He understood the dream in terms of primary identities based on early family roles. His theory did not allow him, however, to even raise the questions of archetypes and archetypal images, except as another name for early childhood experiences in the family. The same is true of other clinical theories, such as object-relations theory, that are based on early childhood experiences in the family.

25. This dream is reported in Hall, *Clinical Uses of Dreams*, 327–335.

26. See appendix.

27. Jung, *CW* 14.

28. M-L von Franz, *Individuation in Fairy Tales* (Zurich: Spring, 1977).

29. Cf. Hannah Arendt, *The Life of the Mind* (New York: Harcourt, Brace, Jovanovich, 1971) 24: "our mental apparatus, though it can withdraw from *present* appearances, remains geared to Appearance."

30. Jung himself believed that such anomalies are actual. See *CW* 8, pars. 816–968.

31. Jung, *Memories, Dreams, Reflections*, p. 296.

32. M-L von Franz, *On Dreams and Death: A Jungian Interpretation* (Boston: Shambhala, 1986).

33. Ibid., 64.

34. J.B. Rhine, "The Parapsychology of Religion: A New Branch of Inquiry," *Journal of Texas and Oklahoma Societies of Psychical Research* 1–23 (1976–77) 9–10.

35. K. Nishitani, *Religion and Nothingness* (Berkeley: University of California Press, 1982) 77–118. Bernstein has discussed the fear of non-being as the anxiety peculiar to the Cartesian "I think,

therefore I am" in *Beyond Objectivity and Relativism* (Philadelphia: University of Pennsylvania Press, 1988).

36. The notion that all things arise in a mysterious manner from emptiness corresponds with Jung's observation that many spontaneously produced modern mandalas have empty centers.

37. For an illuminating exploration of the Christian concept of *Kenosis* in relation to the Buddhist *Sunyata*, see Masao Abe, "Kenotic God and Dynamic Sunyata," in *The Emptying God*, edited by John B. Cobb and Christopher Ives, *Faith Meets Faith Series* (New York: Orbis, 1990).

38. Harold Coward, *Jung and Eastern Thought* (New York: State University of New York Press, 1985).

39. Jung, *CW* 9ii.

40. Polly Young-Eisendrath and I have reviewed several theories of the self. Dr. Young-Eisendrath and I are urging that Jung's Self theory be considered along with other theories in the endless competition for models of the self that are adequate to "the nature of things." See Polly Young-Eisendrath and James A. Hall, eds. *The Book of the Self* (New York: New York University Press, 1987). Elsewhere we have argued that Jung's Self is a profound constructionist theory, not a postulated foundational theory, although we have some differences of opinion about the exact nature of the Self. In Jung's view, as we read it, human beings profoundly construct what they accept as "reality." This idea is commonplace in psychoanalytic practice, where one sometimes hears the old joke: "Neurotics build castles in the air, but psychotics *live* in them." Everyone at some time in life discovers that the appearances which have seemed real have a hidden depth: but that, too, may eventually appear as illusion. It is this paradoxical Self that Jung saw as the organizing center of the human psyche. See Young-Eisendrath and Hall, *Jung's Self Psychology* (New York: Guilford, 1990).

41. In Polanyi's view, I am making a personal statement (the reality of the Self) with universal intent (the expectation that other observers who look at the same phenomena will find the Archetypal Self a compelling model).

42. Cf. John Perry, *Roots of Renewal in Myth and Madness* (San Francisco: Josey-Bass, 1976).
43. Jung, *CW* 13, 1–56.
44. Jung, *CW* 8, pars. 816–968, 969–997; *CW* 18, pars. 1193–1212.
45. See "Synchronicity: An Acausal Connecting Principle" (1952) in *The Structure and Dynamics of the Psyche*, CW 8, 1960.
46. See H. B. Crasilneck and Hall, *Clinical Hypnosis: Principles and Applications* (New York: Grune & Stratton, 1985, 2nd edition).
47. Michael Polanyi, *Personal Knowledge*, (Chicago: University of Chicago Press, 1958).
48. Ibid., 284.
49. Ibid.
50. Ibid., 285.
51. Ibid., 376–377.
52. Ibid., 328–331.
53. *Jung, CW* 2.
54. Jung, *CW* 6, par. 706.
55. Jung, *CW* 18, par. 150.
56. Ibid., par. 789.
57. Polanyi, *Personal Knowledge*, 286.
58. Ibid., 139–142.

Bibliography

Arendt, H. *The Life of the Mind.* New York: Harcourt, Brace & Jovanovich, 1971.

Bernstein, R. *Beyond Objectivity and Relativism.* Philadelphia: University of Pennsylvania Press, 1988.

Boss, M. *The Analysis of Dreams.* New York: Philosophical Library, 1958.

Coward, H. *Jung and Eastern Thought.* New York: State University of New York Press, 1985.

Crasilneck, H.B. and Hall, J.A. *Clinical Hypnosis: Principles and Applications.* 2nd ed. New York: Grune & Stratton, 1985.

DeBecker, R. *The Understanding of Dreams, or the Machinations of the Night.* trans. H. Heron. London: Allen & Unwin, 1968.

Fordham, M. *The Objective Psyche.* London: Routledge & Kegan Paul, 1958.

Govinda, A. "Mandalas." Videotape Lecture. Dallas: Sangreal Foundation, 1972.

Hall, J.A. and Gruver, D. "Religion and Medicine: the Opinions of Medical Students." *New Physician.* Vol. 9, No. 112 (1960): 41–43.

Hall, J.A. "Dreams Clue the Psychiatrist to Patients' Readiness to Change." *Roche Report.* Vol. 4, No. 20 (December 1, 1974).

———. "Editorial." *Journal of the Texas Society* for Psychical Research. (1974–1975a): 36.

———. "Introduction: Symposium on Parapsychology and Religion." *Journal of the Texas Society for Psychical Research and the Oklahoma Society for Psychical Research.* (1977–1978): 11a.

———. "Parapsychology, Religion, and Depth Psychology," *Journal of the Texas Society for Psychical Research and the Oklahoma Society for Psychical Research.* (1977–1978): 36–46.

———. *Clinical Uses of Dreams: Jungian Interpretations and Enactments.* New York: Grune & Stratton, 1977.

———. "Religious Images in Dreams." *Journal of Religion and Health.* Vol. 18 (1979): 327–335.

———. "Jungian Theory in Religious Counseling." *Proceedings of the Society for the Scientific Study of Religion.* (Southwest). Houston: Rice Institute Meeting, 1980.

———. "Polanyi and Jungian Psychology: Dream-ego and Waking-ego." *Journal of Analytical Psychology.* Vol. 27 (1982a): 239–254.

———. "The Use of Dreams and Dream Interpretation in Analysis." *Jungian Analysis.* Ed. M. Stein. LaSalle & London: Open Court, 1982b.

———. *Jungian Dream Interpretations: A Handbook of Theory and Practice.* Toronto: Inner City Books, 1983.

———. "Pseudo-objectivity as a Defence Mechanism: Polanyi's Concept of Dynamo-Objective Coupling." *Journal of the American Academy of Psychoanalysis.* Vol. 12, No. 2 (April, 1984): 199–209.

———. *The Jungian Experience: Analysis and Individuation.* Toronto: Inner City Books, 1986a.

———. "Personal Transformation: The Inner Image of Individuation." *Betwixt and Between: Patterns of Masculine and Feminine Initiation.* Ed. L.C. Madhi et al. LaSalle, Il: Open Court, 1987a.

———. "A Jungian Perspective on Parapsychology: Implications for Science and Religion." *Parapsychology, Philosophy, and Religious Concepts: Proceedings of an International Conference* (Rome, August 23–24, 1985). New York: Parapsychology Foundation, Inc., 20–32.

———. "Parental Imagos: Their Repair and Restitution in Dreams." *The Family: Cultural and Archetypal Dimensions.* Proceedings of the National Conference of Jungian Analysts (October 20–23, 1988). San Francisco: C.G. Jung Institute, 94–98.

Jung, C.G. and von Franz, M-L eds. *Man and His Symbols.* New York: Doubleday, 1964.

Jung, C.G. *The Collected Works of C.G. Jung.* Bollingen Series XX, 20 vols., trans. R.F.C. Hull (except vol. 2, translated by Leopold Stein in collaboration with Diana Riviere), eds. H. Read, M. Fordham, G. Adler. Executive ed. Wm. McGuire. London: Routledge & Kegan Paul, 1953-1979.

――――. *Memories, Dreams, Reflections.* New York: Pantheon, 1961.

Keeler, E.C. *Secrets of the Cuna Earthmother: A Comparative Study of Ancient Religions.* New York: Exposition Press, 1960.

Meckel, D.J. and Moore, R.L. *Self and Liberation: The Jung-Buddhism Dialogue.* Jung and Spirituality Series. New York: Paulist Press, 1992.

Meier, C.A. *Ancient Incubation and Modern Psychotherapy.* Trans. M. Curtis. Evanston: Northwestern University Press, 1967.

Moore, R.L. and Meckel, D.J. *Jung and Christianity in Dialogue: Faith, Feminism, and Hermeneutics.* New York: Paulist Press, 1990.

Newton, P.M. "Recalled Dream Content and the Maintenance of Body Image," Doctoral Dissertation, Columbia University, 1969.

Nishitani, K. *Religion and Nothingness.* Berkeley: University of California Press, 1982.

Perry, J. *Roots of Renewal in Myth and Madness.* San Francisco: Josey-Bass, 1976.

Polanyi, M. *Personal Knowledge.* Chicago: University of Chicago Press, 1958.

Rhine, J.B. "The Parapsychology of Religion: A New Branch of Inquiry." *Journal of the Texas Society for Psychical Research and the Oklahoma Society for Psychical Research.* 1977-1978, 1-23.

Stein, M. *Jung's Treatment of Christianity.* Wilmette, Ill: Chiron Publications, 1985.

―――― and Moore, R.L., eds. *Jung's Challenge to Contemporary Religion.* Wilmette Ill: Chiron Publications, 1987.

von Franz, M-L. *Individuation in Fairy Tales.* Zurich: Spring, 1977.

――――. *On Dreams and Death: A Jungian Interpretation.* Boston: Shambhala, 1986.

Young-Eisendrath, P. and Hall, J.A., eds. *The Book of the Self.* New York: New York University Press, 1987.

――――, eds. *Jung's Self Psychology.* New York: Guilford, 1990.

About the Authors

JAMES A. HALL, M.D., is Clinical Associate Professor of Psychiatry at Southwestern Medical School. He is founding president of the Interregional Society of Jungian Analysts, and the C.G. Jung Institute of Dallas. Dr. Hall's works include *Clinical Uses of Dreams* (Grune & Stratton, 1977), *Jungian Dream Interpretation* (Inner City, 1983), *The Jungian Experience* (Inner City, 1986) and *Hypnosis: A Jungian Perspective* (Guilford, 1989).

DANIEL J. MECKEL, M.A., is editor of several works on psychology and spirituality and Managing Editor of the Jung and Spirituality series.